REGIONAL ECOLOGY

The Study of Man's Environment

Other Books by Robert E. Dickinson

The Making of Geography, written in collaboration with Dr. O. J. R. Howarth, Secretary of the British Association for the Advancement of Science (two-thirds of the work from 1500 onwards), Oxford University Press, 1932, 258 pages.

The German Lebensraum, Penguin Special, London, 1944, 223 pages, 18 maps.

The Regions of Germany, International Library of Sociology and Social Reconstruction, Routledge and Kegan Paul, London, 1945, 175 pages, 29 maps.

City, Region, and Regionalism, International Library of Sociology and Social Reconstruction, Routledge and Kegan Paul, London, 1947, 327 pages, 75 maps.

The West European City: A Geographical Interpretation, Routledge and Kegan Paul, London, 1952, 580 pages, 130 maps, 16 plates.

A Geography of Germany, Methuen, London, 700 pages, 124 maps, 32 plates.

Population Problem in Southern Italy, Syracuse University Press, New York, 1955, 116 pages, 23 maps, 6 tables, 22 plates.

City and Region: A Geographical Interpretation, Routledge and Kegan Paul, London, 1964, 588 pages, 125 maps.

The City Region in Western Europe, Routledge and Kegan Paul, London, 1967, 305 pages, 64 maps.

Makers of Modern Geography, Routledge and Kegan Paul, London, 1969, 305 pages.

REGIONAL ECOLOGY
The Study of Man's Environment

ROBERT E. DICKINSON

JOHN WILEY & SONS, INC.
New York London Sydney Toronto

Library of Congress Catalog Card Number: 71-123739
ISBN 0-471-21288-1

Printed in the United States of America

10 9 8 7 6 5 4 3 2 1

TO

Carl O. Sauer

and

Lewis Mumford

PREFACE

The regional concept refers to the segregation of phenomena on the Earth's surface in spatial groupings, that may be described as unique or specific groupings and as worldwide repetitive or generic groupings. These earthbound phenomena fall into three categories: physical (or natural); biotic; and human; each leading into distinct, although interdependent, fields of enquiry. I shall concentrate in this book on the human aspect, in which the physical Earth and its cover of life forms are interpreted from the standpoint of their significance to Man. This study was described in 1887 by Sir Halford MacKinder, the founder of geography in Britain (at the age of 26) as the study of the "local variations" of environment, as processed by Nature and modified by Man, such variations forming a spatial hierarchy of "different orders." This ecological approach to the study of environment is a matter of increasing public concern, and urgently needs clarification as to objectives, expertise, and utility, in the shaping of the physical Earth as the habitat of Man. Such is the purpose of these pages.

It is generally agreed, especially among continental scholars, that the regional concept is the core of geography. Its meaning and expertise are of profound importance in education and current affairs. However, geographers in the Universities of the Anglo American world in particular reject what they condemn as the "traditional" approach to the regional concept as a summation of areal data that results in a "quagmire of eclecticism." Although this rejection, in these terms, is justified, it is aimed at a procedure that has been outdated for a generation. The regional concept, especially in Europe, has advanced far in the past 40 years; a period that covers the professional career of the present writer, who rejected the concept his younger contemporaries now condemn at the beginning of his career in 1925. It was gratifying to be told recently by a French geographer that geographical research today is "bursting out all over" and is fertilizing other fields of enquiry, both in the natural and social sciences. However, the essential question remains as to what is the distinctive core of geography, with respect to its conceptual structure, expertise, and problems.

This book seeks to present answers to this question by dealing with the essentials of its expertise in measurement, mapping and interpretation of Man's environment. It does not presume to set limits to the work of any researchers; their efforts will be judged at the bar of scholarship. It does emphatically insist, however, that the regional concept demands disciplinary training at the University level from the undergraduate course to the final doctorate examination. Moreover, there is urgent need of a much wider appreciation, and therefore, a clear understandable explanation of what the regional concept is all about, and its significance in education, research, and public affairs. I am not seeking to define a discipline, but to explore the meaning and value of a concept.

The reader should know of the writer's background, since this affects the whole approach of the book. I am British by birth, training and early professional experience (University of London, 1928–1947 under C. B. Fawcett). For 20 years I have been a resident (permanently from 1947 to 1958, and intermittently since 1958) in the United States (Syracuse University, 1947–1958, University of Leeds, England since 1958, and Visiting Professor at the University of California, 1960–1961, and for semesters subsequently at Universities of Washington, Minnesota, Nebraska, Kansas State, Arizona [Tucson], and Laval, Quebec). However, my area of research, with continuous personal contacts for nearly 40 years, has been France and Germany. My background thus has a very strong continental flavor. I am also aware from long experience of the advantages and shortcomings of education in general in both Britain and the United States. I am now a permanent resident in the United States and seek to play a part through this book in the great educational challenge that confronts this nation.

I stated in a concluding paragraph of my *Makers of Modern Geography*, London, 1969, that "the purpose and concepts of geography, and the objectives of its practitioners, as teachers and researchers, need to be clearly and boldly articulated." This book is an attempt to meet this challenge. It seeks to select what is relevant in the regional concept in current trends, especially in continental Europe; and is inevitably in large measure a personal record of research and writing for a period of over 40 years.

There has been a remarkable international impact in recent years of the quantitative analysis of spatial variables, under the banner of "regional science." Although unquestionably its expertise, as we shall recognize in the book, is indispensable to the regional concept, much of its concern is more than marginal to it. Its approach is an essential means, not an end, to furtherance of the regional concept. Moreover, the study of individual spatial distributions was categorically rejected by geographers about 50 years ago. The interpretation of the regional concept in this book is held by leading scholars on both sides of the Atlantic and is, if I may dare the phrase, traditionally based. This consensus was revealed to the writer conclusively at a 3 day seminar at the University of Saarbrücken, convened by Professor J. Schmithüsen, in April, 1965. Some 20 of the leading geographers in Western Europe participated. In spite of wide divergences of interest, there was common agreement on the fact that they were all concerned with the study of "geographic complexes" of physical, biotic, and human phenomena. Indeed, I presented the theme of this book as a springboard for one day's discussion. This is my interpretation of the regional concept. It is not intended for a narrow geographic fraternity; but for natural and social scientists, and city and regional planners. In Western Europe I would anticipate that it would reach a still wider reading public. I hope this will be the case in the United States.

Robert E. Dickinson

Tucson, Arizona
February, 1970

CONTENTS

Part III PRACTICE

PART I

HISTORY

Chapter 1

INTRODUCTION

In these modern days, the traditional claim of geography to spatial omniscience cannot be justified. Geography has often been referred to as a mother of sciences. Geomorphology, oceanography, hydrology, climatology and plant geography were developed from geographical studies and now stand as separate disciplines in the realm of the natural sciences. During this century a great deal of attention has been given to the social sciences. Ecology, chorology, regional science, ekistics (defined by C. Doxiadis as "the scientific study of human settlement") are synonyms that have been suggested in recent years. Although geography finds recognition in the United States at the level of the national academies and similar organizations as an earth science, it receives dubious recognition among the social sciences. However, public demand for research, teaching and interpretation of current affairs makes its approach of increasing concern at all levels of learning. The traditional field of geography is vast and attracts an increasing number of students with diverse interests and qualifications —geologists, meteorologists, botanists, economic historians, social scientists, and others. As knowledge and know-how increase, and the narrowly specialized scientific approach becomes more sophisticated, the diversity of competence increases. Historians, chemists, biologists, and geologists are confronted with exactly the same problem. It must be accepted as a scientific trend and need of our time. A thorough reevaluation of the conceptual framework of the discipline of geography is essential. This is not a question of defining watertight compartments or what has been called "arid definition." It is a question of clarifying content, objectives, and expertise. Physical and social scientists want to know what distinctive contribution the geographer has to offer to the realm of knowledge. They need to know the essential expertise of the geographer.

Changes in the scope and purpose of geography have materialized largely as a result of the scientific progress in the sciences and the humanities since the middle of the eighteenth century. Knowledge of the character and distribution of physical and human phenomena throughout the world was greatly increased through the work of scientific explorers. There was a vast accumulation of facts bearing on all aspects of science in the nineteenth century: Such activities included improvements in cartographic methods; the initiation and, in many countries, the completion, of national topographic surveys; the production of maps based on general surveys of the unexplored continental interiors, improvement in astronomical observations and methods of land measurement, and the collection of data under the auspices of governments and learned societies.

During the latter half of the eighteenth and the first half of the nineteenth century empiricism was, for two main reasons, the keynote to scientific progress. First, this is the first stage in the systematization of new facts, in advance of the deduction of general laws. Second, the old idea of the origin of the earth, known as catastrophism, as opposed to uniformitarianism, was still generally held. This was reflected in the predominance of the old cosmogony which, based upon the evident adaptation of all forms of life to environment, argued that divine design was responsible for the apparently perfect order and harmony on the earth.

The theory of evolution, brought to fruition by Darwin in the middle of the nineteenth century, breathed new life into the scientific spirit in the second half of the century. In particular, it resulted in the introduction of causal as opposed to teleological interpretation into the earth sciences and humanities. Its basic tenets in the field of life phenomena were natural selection through struggle with the natural environment, inheritance of acquired characteristics, and survival of the fittest. Transfer of these ideas to human societies led to a mechanistic association of cause and effect, based fundamentally on the dictates of the natural environment.

The first half of the twentieth century witnessed a more critical study of human relations with environment. It became recognized that Man is not a creature of his environment, but, through conscious endeavor, according to his stage of development and social heritage, adjusts himself to it. This approach results in a new kind of spatial synthesis, which will be examined in the following chapters.

The interpretation of the adjustment of Man to Nature has its core in the small area of a distinct local environment. Environment was still thought of a generation ago as an abstraction of natural conditions. Today it is evaluated as a complex of physical and cultural phenomena. Chorography, to use Ptolemy's term, was still current in geographical parlance at the end of the last century. It is still evident in the German term for the smallest geographical unit (*chore* derived from the Greek word *choros*). It is concerned with the explanatory description of the regional (that is, areal or geographic) variations of the earth's surface. In this sense geography is the chorological science, that is, it is the regional science, of the surface of the earth as the human habitat.

The advancement of geographical study was fundamentally dependent upon the extension of knowledge and the mapping, of lands, seas and peoples of the earth. Great advances took place during the nineteenth century; but, large areas of the earth were still vaguely known in 1900. Astonishing advances have been made in this century.

The end of the eighteenth century witnessed the establishment of an independent state on the eastern seaboard of America, the first settlement on the southeastern tip of Australia, and, the firm establishment of European settlement at the Cape. The great continental interiors were unknown. The early years of the nineteenth century witnessed the advent of the sailing ship and, after mid-century, the steamship. The second half witnessed the exploration of the continental interiors by the trader, explorer and scientist, then by the railroad and the expansion of the frontiers of human settlement. The spirit of scientific enquiry sent out a new kind of explorer for the collection of data about distant lands and their peoples, beginning with the scientific advances of the eighteenth century in what has been called "the age of measurement? The philosophic ideas of Nature and Man of the late eighteenth century continued into the nineteenth century. Though ideas of gradual change were replacing ideas of catastrophism and "positivism" was replacing "romanticism", it was not until the sixties that Darwin's theory of evolution permeated the interpretation of the natural world and Man's place within it.

In this great century of widening horizons, with its period of maximum impact in the "wonderful years" of the sixties, it was natural that there should be a great increase in the accumulation of facts about nature and society. Explorers of all kinds were expanding the realm of knowledge about lands and peoples. Widely dispersed and incredibly long and difficult routes were taken by explorers through uninhabited grasslands, deserts, and forests. It was not until the latter half of the century that the front of close agricultural settlement expanded in America and Australia and, with more limited extent, in South America and South Africa. It was not until this time that an organized body of knowledge about the lands and peoples of the earth began to take shape, alongside allied disciplines in the natural sciences.

Geographical societies were founded at this time to promote exploration and to advance the use of the statistics that were being amassed by the new generation of census takers. Indeed, geography as the mother of sciences of the earth, after draining materials and ideas in abundance from explorers and academicians, found it necessary, when emerging in the Universities as a distinct modern discipline around 1900, more vigorously to define its field. The promotion of geography in the last decades of the nineteenth century, owed most to geologists and ethnographers. Its range was so catholic that all concerned with lands and peoples—geologists, oceanographers, botanists and ethnographers—either considered themselves "geographers" or were appointed to new chairs of geography in the Universities. These men, after the days of Humboldt and Ritter, who were among the great scholars of the pre-evolutionary epoch in the first half of the century, had to put their new house in order as a University study, so as to establish its position in the realm of knowledge. This was begun in Germany, where speculation on the scope and problems of geography has been a subject of concern from the middle of the eighteenth century until our day—a period of two hundred years.

Prodigious strides in the mapping of the earth and the distribution of its peoples have been made in this century. Most of the world is now mapped from ground surveys and from manned aircraft. In the last few years the whole earth has been mapped on a large scale from crewless satellites. Scientific observers are engaged in accurate and regular observations throughout the year in underground shelters at altitudes of 9,000 feet at the South Pole. We live on the brink of a new era. Concepts and training are in need of sharper and often drastic revision in the light of present trends and future requirements.

Chapter 2

THE BEGINNINGS

1. STRABO AND PTOLEMY

The first recorded use of the word "geography" is in the lost work of Eratosthenes in the third century before Christ. It is derived from the Greek *geo* meaning the earth, and *grapho* meaning I write. Geography literally means, therefore, writing about, or description of, the earth. Its practitioners since the days of the Greek poet Homer have written about the lands, seas and peoples of the habited world—the Greek *ecumene*—and speculated about lands and peoples beyond the range of their knowledge. The known world was limited to the lands around the Central Sea, the Mediterranean. The discovery of the new world and voyages to the Orient extended the horizons. But even at the end of the nineteenth century, a mere two generations ago, knowledge of places throughout most of the world was woefully inadequate to permit reliable generalizations about locations and spatial relationships. The advances in these respects over the past hundred years have been remarkable. However, for two thousand years, the written records (required in the absence of mapping techniques) and theories have far outrun the available facts to support them. The translators of classical tracts almost invariably ignore this, and pay far too much attention to the wrong orientation of a river or the shape of a land, than to the concepts these intelligent and discriminating scholars were trying to develop.

Classical scholars, represented by Strabo and Ptolemy, believed that geography was concerned with the location, attributes, and interconnections of places of the world as a whole; chorography with the interrelations of places as distinct districts; topography with places as discrete units. These terms are based on the Greek roots *geo* (earth) *choros* (district or area), and *topos* (place). All three are in active usage in English to this day. They were redefined in the famous writings of Bernard Varenius in the mid-seventeenth and by the German philosopher, I. Kant, in the late eighteeenth centuries. The single uniting idea behind this conceptual framework is what Strabo described as "the natural attributes of place" within a framework of relations to other places on the surface of the earth. No matter how sophisticated modern concepts and procedures have become today, this is the essential and unique content of the regional concept. It remains firmly fixed in popular parlance to this day. Cosmography, as well as the other three terms, was widely used by writers in the Renaissance period. Its practitioners considered the earth's properties that were derived from its position as a body in space. The shape, size and divisions of the earth were its content—latitude and longitude, movements of the sun, variations in the length of day and night (the seasons), and Aristotle's torrid, temperate and frigid zones. Strabo pointed out that cosmographical ideas were necessary to a description of the properties and interrelations of places. Its derivative—Cartography—remains to this day a sophisticated study in its own right.

2. VARENIUS AND CLUVERIUS

This mode of organization of knowledge of places made little progress as a body of knowledge in the so-called "dark" and "middle ages". During the Renaissance Period classical ideas were revived. The inaccurate and outmoded ideas of Ptolemy and Strabo survived into the nineteenth century indeed, Aristotle's notion of torrid, temperate and frigid zones, though cosmographically sound, has little support in the realities of temperature though his usage widely persists to our day. The chief Renaissance scholars followed classical ideas and presentation and theirs were considered standard works for about one hundred years. Sebastian Munster, in particular, described lands and peoples in the same manner as Strabo, and, indeed, reproduced much of the latter's material. His book went through 46 editions and appeared in six languages.

A big step forward was taken in the mid-seventeenth century by Bernard Varenius in Holland. His work was first published in 1650 (at the age of 28), with the title *Geographia generalis*. The study is divided into two parts, general or universal and special or particular.

> "We call that *Universal Geography* which considers the whole Earth in general and explains its properties without regard to particular countries. But *Special or Particular Geography* describes the Constitution and Situation of each single country by itself, viz., Chorographical, which describes countries of a considerable extent; or Topographical, which gives a view of some piece or small tract of the Earth."

This conceptual statement, and the way in which Varenius develops it, bring us to the modern threshold of the regional concept. This prompts two questions. First, what is meant by a *country* and by a *tract* and by "a considerable extent"? Second, what shall be the attributes of places that shall be assembled, interpreted, and presented as giving to such an area its distinctive character?

Two other outstanding writers of geographies in this period who pursued thoroughly contrasted procedures were Nathaniel Carpenter in England and Philip Cluverius in Germany. Carpenter sought to arrive at generalizations concerning the location and groupings of places, especially in reference to human characteristics. Cluverius, on the other hand, continued in the time-honored tradition of Strabo by writing lengthy descriptions of countries (with much material directly derived from Strabo, Caesar, and others). He also maintained the Ptolomaic definitions of geography, chorography and topography. These works were standards until the middle of the eighteenth century.

Immanuel Kant (1724-1804), the German philosopher, lectured on "physical geography" in the University of Königsberg. He reflected the philosophy of his time by including Man within this field, since he viewed the physical world accessible to experience and reason, known as natural philosophy, as opposed to Man's own purpose and being, which was known as moral philosophy. He regarded history as the sequence of events in time and geography as the arrangement of facts in space. Physical geography he regarded as the basis not only of history but also of "all other possible geographies." These included mathematical, moral, political, mercantile and theological geography. Physical geography thus covered the earth's surface, its cover of plants and animals, and the presence and works of Man. The "other geographies" were concerned with the difference from place to place of the attributes of Man.

Kant followed the Ptolemaic approach. However, one major difference is that the classical geographers put primary emphasis on the areal divisions of the earth. Kant, on the other hand, was rather concerned with the orderly spatial arrangement of particular sets of phenomena. These two approaches have been recently described as theoretical-deductive and empirical-descriptive. The first seeks to establish theories *ab initio* relevant to the location and spatial groupings of places and to establish laws and make deductions on the basis of the laws. The second seeks to develop modes of description of particular groupings of nations and peoples in terms of lands, seas, countries, and places. It does not search for laws; rather how the local associations of phenomena account for the character of a place and its relations of similiarity and grouping with other places. The contrast and conflict of these two approaches have become more marked as knowledge of the surface of the earth has increased over the past hundred years. This will become evident to the reader in the following pages.

3. COMPILATIONS ABOUT 1800

The latter half of the eighteenth and the first half of the nineteenth centuries, a period of about one hundred years, ending with the year 1859, witnessed a remarkable growth of knowledge on which background changes in the regional concept should be evaluated. Four trends in this period are relevant to our theme: progress of exploration and mapping; development of the relations of human societies to the world of Nature; the idea of an order of natural units; the first attempts to arrange the facts of Man and Nature into categories, and to seek classification and origins. Each of these may be succinctly noted.

The outline of the world, inside about latitudes 60° North and South, was correctly mapped, after several hundred years frustration by the ill-conceived estimates of Ptolemy of the distortion of lands over the earth. Vast areas of the continental interiors were still virtually unknown and data scarce and, therefore, entirely unmapped. Trails were cut across these vastnesses in the first half of the nineteenth century, nevertheless, this situation still remained essentially true in 1859. Great advances were made, however, in human knowledge, with respect to the collection of facts and the formulation of theories. First steps were taken in the classification of plants and human races, and there were new developments in the philosophy and course of human history. The view of catastrophism dominated the scholastic interpretation of both Nature and Man. However, evidence was being slowly accumulated for the view of uniformitarianism, particularly from the works of British geologists such as Playfair, Hutton and Lyell—a trend that grew into the remarkable impact of Charles Darwin's *Origin of Species* in 1859. It was customary to regard the world as embracing the world of the inner man, known (and surviving to this day) as moral philosophy, and the world of the outer man, the world of observation and experience, known as natural philosophy. Further, there was the philosophical view of the concordant or sympathetic interrelations of the environment and Man, as determined by Divine Intent, for good or ill, that pervaded thought until towards the end of the century.

Mammoth compilations were made of the lands and peoples of the world in so far as known at the time. The most remarkable of these was contained in over 40 volumes of "natural history" written towards the end of the eighteenth century by Count Buffon in France. Compilations of lands and peoples were also made at this time in Britain (Pinkerton), the United States (Morse), Germany (Ritter) and France (Malte-Brun). These works are important landmarks in the assessment of geographical knowledge. They reveal very clearly that in the early nineteenth century such writings about the surface of the earth considered all that was known about it. They were disorderly, descriptive compilations, in the manner of Strabo. They revealed an abysmal ignorance of most of the lands on earth and of the history and character of human societies, and no sense of order as to sequence or cause.

A further trend concerns the mode of classification of terrestial data pertaining to the differences between and grouping of places on the earth. New ideas of arrangement were gradually appearing. There is first the conception of the "natural division" of land. It was widely supposed that drainage basins, bordered by more or less clearly defined ranges, could be used as such a basis. Secondly, various authors, notably Germans, in descriptive writings of lands and peoples, customarily used the crazy quilt of changing political divisions as units for description. These were found to be notoriously inadequate (especially in the German lands) because of their impermanence and lack of accord with other distributions that ran right across political divisions. They began to think of "lands" as homogeneous areas of associated phenomena, and, most important, regarded them—very inadequately because of the lack of data to support them—as falling into areas in a hierarchical order. The sequence began with the visible landscape, reaching as far as the horizon, and thence, beyond the range of vision embracing major continental divisions, that in turn make up the earth's surface as a whole.

Some divisions were vaguely based on a diversity of spatially arranged phenomena. One thought that emerged to cope with this difficulty was to confine attention to the visible areal variants of the surface of the earth. Another thought suggested the exclusion of the works of Man and confinement of attention to the areal variables of the physical earth. A third thought attacked the "holistic" view, that regarded an area as distinct in virtue of the total spatial association of the phenomena within it, that so clearly reflected the philosophical attitude of the period. It was argued by a few that the only scientific method of collecting, classifying, and explaining, spatially distributed phenomena was to attend exclusively to particular sets of phenomena. This view, therefore, rejected the use of areas as vehicles of descriptive transmission, for in fact all spatially arranged phenomena do not stop at the boundary of an arbitrarily selected division.

These were the ideas current in the early nineteenth century and they are clearly reflected in the works of two of the greatest scholars of this era. Both were Germans, Alexander Von Humboldt, a natural philosopher, explorer and researcher, and Carl Ritter, professor of geography in the University of Berlin for 40 years till his death in 1859, essentially a student of the history of Man, but the persistent practitioner and exponent of a "new geography." The works of these two men have been commented on elsewhere and we shall limit ourselves here to certain general conclusions regarding their works and ideas in relation to the regional concept.

4. HUMBOLDT AND RITTER

Alexander Von Humboldt (1769-1859) and Carl Ritter (1779-1859) were both outstanding scholars with an international reputation. Their ideas and purposes, although formulated before the great impact of evolutionary thought in the sixties, and before the enormous extension of exploration into the continental interiors in the latter half of the century, have continued to this day as guide-posts to the purpose of the regional concept. Both men died in 1859, the same year as the publication of Charles Darwin's *Origin of Species.* Their work is the culmination of the remarkable growth of human knowledge in the preceding hundred years. Humboldt was a natural scientist, and one of the world's first scientific explorers. He wandered for five years, from high Andean peaks to the forests and savannas of the Orinoco. His methods and records were acknowledged by Darwin as one of his main sources of data and inspiration. Ritter was essentially a cultural historian, with his deepest roots in classical antiquity—a fact that clearly emerged in the researches of his immediate followers. Ritter was also essentially a bibliophile and a teacher during his tenure as professor of geography at the University of Berlin from 1819 to 1859. Humboldt, after his South American years, lived and worked in Paris for about 25 years, and then adjourned to Berlin, where, with the patronage of the King of Prussia, he was able to pursue his researches and write his great work on the *Cosmos.* He was always a researcher and minor diplomatist, never a University teacher. Yet both these men shared the same philosophic background and had great respect for each other's works.

The concepts of both Humboldt and Ritter, as revealed in their massive substantive researches, spell the culmination of the approach to human knowledge in the period immediately preceding the impact of Darwinism in the second half of the nineteenth century. Details of their lives and works may be read in the writer's *Makers of Modern Geography,* (London, 1969). We shall summarize here the basic concepts held by both these scholars. They reflect what may be regarded as the culmination of the "holistic" philosophy that was generally held in their era.

1. They regarded geography as an empirical science, based on inductive procedures, leading from particular places to generalizations about the location of the attributes of places, rather than a science based on deduction from *a priori* theories. Geographic study moved from one observation to another regarding the location and attributes of places on the earth's surface. Although Ritter believed that there were "general laws" conditioning such distributions, he was in no hurry to formulate them. This is abundantly evident in the enormous, but unfinished, compilation of the 19 volumes of the *Erdkunde.* Humboldt, on the other hand, looked always for generalizations regarding particular sets of phenomena he had under observation.
2. There is a coherence in the spatial distribution and spatial interconnections of terrestrial phenomena. This is described repeatedly by both men as *Zusammenhang.* Areal phenomena are interrelated so as to form unique associations as "individual units" to use Ritter's term. Geography must rise above "the mere description" that Ritter deplored about the writings of his contemporaries. To avoid the "diversity of origin of its materials," it must have a guiding and distinctive principle. "It uses the whole circle of sciences in order to illustrate its own individuality." He sought for *connections* between sets of phenomena in the same area and between one place and another place. The task of geography, wrote Ritter, is "to get away from mere description to the law of the thing described; to reach not a mere accumulation of facts and figures, but the connection of place with place, the laws which bind together local and general phenomena of the earth's surface." The geographer traces "*causation* and *interdependence* of the (spatially distributed) phenomena, and the *relations* of every one to the country which supplies its conditions of being." These words give the keynote to the approach of both Ritter and Humboldt.
3. Ritter insisted that boundary lines, whether wet, such as rivers, or dry, such as mountain ranges, were "a means toward the real purpose of geography which is the understanding of the content of area." Geography, Ritter maintained, is "the study of the material content of the areas of the earth's surface." It is thus concerned with objects on the earth's surface as they exist together in space. To pursue this end, Humboldt studied particular sets of

phenomena in their areal relations with other phenomena. Ritter, on the other hand, studied the content of areas as a totality, and deliberately deferred broad conclusions until later.

4. Humboldt and Ritter held to the philosophical concept of "holism," with respect to the relevance of the Earth to Man. Ritter wrote that the purpose of his life's work, the *Erdkunde,* was "to present the most important geographic physical conditions of the earth's surface in their coherent interrelation *(Naturzusammenhang)* in terms of its most essential characters and main outlines, especially as the fatherland of the peoples in its most manifold influence on humanity, developing in body and mind." However this, he claimed, was *not* an exclusive concern with Man. "Independent of Man, the Earth is also without him, and before him, the scene of natural phenomena; the law of its formation cannot proceed from Man. In a science of the Earth, the Earth itself must be asked for its laws." The dilemma of today is presented by this double viewpoint in the study of the face of the earth, for today there is a group of well-established disciplines concerned with the observation of phenomena all over the earth that are concerned with natural phenomena as ends in themselves, but not in terms of their relevance to human societies.

5. The concept of the unique and distinct territorial area *(Individuen)* was a main contribution to knowledge by Ritter in spite of its inadequacies owing to the woeful lack of necessary data. In his earlier years Ritter adhered to the view of his contemporaries that river basins and their encircling mountain ranges, were "natural units" of various orders, into which the earth's surface may be divided. It was later that he made the search for such units the objective of his work. In 1806 he wrote—"Every naturally bounded area is a unity in respect of climate, production, culture, population and history." This view he later changed by the idea that this could not be accepted as a matter of faith, but must be the objective of scientific investigation. This scientific approach, emerging from a holistic philosophy, is eminently characteristic as a driving force of the works of Humboldt. Ritter came to regard the "geographical entity" *(Individuen)* not as something given by a natural framework, but as something to be discovered in the physionomy of the Earth. He recognized the major natural divisions of each continent on a *deductive* basis. The Earth was an

organic entity *(organische Einheit)*, consisting of major continental divisions *(Erdteile)* of the highest geographical order. Each of these areas is a complex of individual units *(Ländersysteme)*, which he sought to build inductively from the smallest recognizable units. The ways in which the various sets of phenomena (for example, vegetation and climate) are spatially interconnected and interdependent generically he was never clear about. Ritter recognized no basic difference between the study of the content of particular areas, and the study of worldwide distributions. They were for him different sides of the same coin, general geography dealing with the character, typology and location of different sets of terrestrial phenomena, regional geography dealing with the unique content of particular areas.

6. Finally, while Ritter became inextricably involved in the distribution and association of earthbound phenomena in particular areas, notably in Africa and southwestern Asia, Humboldt always set out with more limited sights, centered on particular objectives. He sought also to focus upon particular sets of phenomena, not only on their immediate spatial association with other phenomena, but also as forms that had analogues in other areas of the earth, and needed to be typologically classified, located and explained. This was the purpose of his researches in Latin America and Central Asia, and his remarkable contributions to the study of plants, climates and volcanoes.

We would conclude this chapter with a special comment on the work of Humboldt. Em. de Martonne, the distinguished French geographer, wrote as follows of him as far back as 1909.

"Whatever phenomena he studied, relief, temperature, vegetation, Humboldt didn't merely treat each individually as a geologist, meteorologist, or botanist. His philosophical outlook carried him further. It led at once to the observation of other phenomena. He sought causes and distant consequences, even including political and historical facts. Nobody has shown with more precision how man depends on the soil, climate and vegetation, and how vegetation is a function of physical phenomena, and how they are dependent on each other."

De Martonne claims that Humboldt was the first to define and apply two essential principles that make geography a distinct science. He sought not the individual spatially distributed phenomena (plants, temperatures, crops) but the complex of the spatially arranged phenomena, such as an association of plants to form a type of vegetation of which the individual plants formed a part, and without which they could not be understood. He sought to find and explain causes and consequences of spatially arranged phenomena. This is what de Martonne called the *principle of spatial causality.* Humboldt also sought to compare the location and extent of "forms" or groupings of terrestial phenomena. This is what de Martonne called the *principle of general geography.*

Humboldt was a great pioneer and well ahead of his epoch, its philosophy and its data regarding the lands and peoples he sought to locate and explain. He was a "natural philosopher" and a founder of the modern spirit of scientific enquiry. Ritter, on the other hand, had an insatiable interest in primitive and classical history for which, he often alleged, the physical earth served merely as a springboard. As a lone professor of geography he had profound repercussions on his immediate successors who were essentially biased towards classical history. It was nearly a generation before chairs of geography were established in Prussian universities, and even then its leaders were far from reconciliation of their own interests, historical or statistical, with the field they were called on to represent and develop.

Chapter 3

MODERN GROWTH

1. THE ENVIRONMENTAL IMPACT

The theory of evolution as formulated by Charles Darwin in 1859, the concepts of natural selection, the survival of the fittest in the struggle for existence, the inheritance of acquired characteristics, and the determinism of the natural environment, had an immediate and widespread impact upon the natural and life sciences. The transfer of these concepts to the interpretation of human societies led to emphasis of Man's relations to the physical environment. This led to the belief that Nature operated directly on Man through the medium of the processes of natural selection. It was supposed that the physical environment acted on Man by an almost mechanistic procedure of cause and effect. This assumption was apparent in the research of scholars and by the teacher in the school classroom. This is the essential basis of what is described as "environmental determinism," that prevailed for over 50 years beyond the 1860's.

The study of human societies in their environmental settings was exclusively concerned with *place* as the "physical base" and the repetitive lifeforms of plants, animals and Man that could be associated with that base. The rest, in the human and economic fields, was described in 1908 by H. R. Mill, one of the latest British social Darwinists, as "a rubble heap" at the top of the pyramid. The search for direct and persistent correlations between specific physical features and specific repetitive human features was presented by W. M. Davis, the American scholar, to the Royal Geographical Society in 1903 as the scientific key to his "scheme of geography." This is probably the most extreme expression of "environmental determinism," from which emerged such terms as "influence" and "control" by Nature over Man. This is now in general outdated, and I hasten to add, was rejected by Davis himself in the twenties. He kept track of thought in Germany (where he had some of his bitterest enemies) and profited by the contact, in that he came to understand and expound in English more clearly than any of his contemporaries the meaning, purpose and procedure of the regional concept.

2. THE SYSTEMATIC IMPACT

Students of the earth sciences soon began to organize and explain the regional arrangement of the phenomena with which they were expertly concerned. Some sought the differential distribution of particular phenomena in the field-rocks, gravels, sediments, terrace remnants, etc., as evidence for the formulation or rejection of hypotheses. A classic example is Albrecht Penck's work on the phases of the Pleistocene Ice Age with its glacial and interglacial periods, which he derived from the meticulous search for field evidence in the valleys of the Alps. The terms, Gunz, Mindel, Reiss, and Würm are all named after Alpine valleys in which his evidence was best exemplified. Others, however, including Penck himself, sought to determine the terrestrial distribution of sets of phenomena on a local, continental, or worldwide scale. Such were the goals of Suess in his great geological work on "the face of the earth," Hann's treatise on climate (p. 100), and early attempts by Supan and Köppen to collate data and establish generic type of climate. There were also around 1900 many studies, especially in German, of "regional geology," which included surface configuration, stratigraphy, and lithology, of selected areas. There were also studies, large and small, of rainfall, temperature, and vegetation by men such as Herbertson and Mill in Britain, Schimper on plant ecology in Germany, W. M. Davis and others on the physiographic entities of the United States. There were also tentative studies of the regional arrangement of individual sets of human phenomena. These were examined in their physical setting, but it was not by any means argued that this was the only regional determinant. This was evident, for example in the first edition of George Chisholm's *Handbook of Commercial Geography,* published in 1888 in Britain. There was concern in France and Germany with classification, distribution, and explanation of man-made settlement forms (rural and urban functions, forms of architecture, and field systems,) which made very little penetration into either Britain or America where environmental determinism persisted strongly. Studies were also made by "ethnographers" of the distribution of racial types, in terms of specific physical traits of head-shape, hair-texture and skin-color.

This systematic approach was adumbrated by Richthofen in his inaugural address at Leipzig in 1883 and it dominated procedures for some 40 years. The composite geographic study of an area according to Richthofen covered the spatial arrangement of earthbound phenomena, physical, biotic, and human, and these should be examined in terms of their forms, material, genesis and spatial interconnections. He called such study at the descriptive level "chorography." As knowledge accumulated and hypotheses became feasible explanation would naturally enter, and thus the study would rise to the level of "chorology." This approach was later described by Albrecht Penck, who was a young man in Richthofen's audience, as a "storied mansion." Each level of the mansion has different occupants and each level has no connection with the others. Many sets of spatially arranged phenomena in the same area (mansion) are thoroughly, and profitably, examined as ends in themselves. The composite is simply a collection of separate studies each forming a story in the mansion. Each essay demands a special expertise, either from the one writer (architect), dealing with the whole mansion, or a number of contributors whom he invites in as sub-contractors. There is no unique or distinctive theme that welds the whole together as a mansion with a distinctive form. It is a scholarly collection of well constructed ingredients at various levels. The mansion is a rectangular skyscraper, unlike H. R. Mill's environmental pyramid with a residual "rubble heap" at it's apex.

3. THE SURVEY IMPACT

PLACE	Place WORK (natural advantages)	Place FOLK (natives)
Work PLACE (pasture, fields, mine, workshop)	WORK	Work FOLK (industrial)
Folk PLACE (village, home, etc.)	Folk WORK (occupation)	FOLK

A reaction to the environmental emphasis in the manner of social Darwinism was established in Britain by the Scottish biologist, Patrick Geddes, in the first quarter of this century. He recognized that the life of human groups in their environmental aspects was supported by the three legs of a tripod, namely, Place (physical characteristics of the land), Folk (racial and inherited characteristics), and Work (modes of economic activity and support). These three aspects react upon each other in a manner shown by Geddes in one of his famous short-hand diagrams as shown above.

Geddes' approach known as "regional survey" led in two directions in Britain. First, the spatial diagnosis of social situations was used as a guideline to physical planning (especially to the reconstruction of cities). Second, the Place-Work-Folk formula was used as an educational medium, for the assembly of data in the field study of a particular area. A "regional survey" became the basic diagnosis in city and country planning for a generation between the world wars. It was also used as an explanatory device for all kinds of field observation.

The Place, Work and Folk trilogy was transformed by Geddes himself into Geography, Economics and Sociology. Geddes' young assistant, A. J. Herbertson (who, after serving under Mackinder at Oxford, finally became its first professor of geography) transformed it into Environment, Function and Organism. It must be emphasized that Geddes regarded the relations of these three as a mutual interaction in creating the spatial patterns of a society in a particular environmental setting.

This mode of approach clearly stemmed from Frederic Leplay, the French sociologist, a generation earlier, and had its parallels in the work of his successors in France around 1900, notably Demolins and De Tourville. There were those also who associated inherited mental and social traits with specific racial characteristics. This led to a gross exaggeration of the role of race (meaning physical breed) in the social life and attitudes of human groups in their environmental settings. The superiority in traits of leadership and initiative, for example, of the so-called Nordic racial type (tall, fair, long-headed, blue eyes) was emphasized by certain scholars (including H. J. Fleure in his *Human Geography of Western Europe,* published in 1918 in the *Making of the Future* series edited by Geddes.) This vogue reached its peak of exaggeration in the writings of Lothrop Stoddard and Madison Grant in America, who urged the maintenance of the Nordic stock and warned against "the rising tide of color." Concern was also expressed about the high mortality of Nordic stock in urban environments where it was particularly prone to certain diseases such as tuberculosis as compared to other racial stocks. These people were supposed to have highly desirable mental qualities and traits of leadership, which would eugenically be a deplorable social loss. Such ideas were continued by the nationalistic policies of the Nazis and are currently propagated in the equally absurd pejorative notion of "Anglo-Saxon" that emanates from France.

4. THE LANDSCAPE IMPACT

There was a strong trend in the early 1900's in Germany and France moving away from the environmental approach to a more clearly defined focus and standard of relevance in regional study. This focus was sought in the visible landscape scene, which should be studied with the same objectivity of classification and genesis as was fully established in the study of landforms, climates, and vegetation. Such study demands an appreciation of the individual phenomena of the landscape, but reaches further for the areal distribution of the same phenomena in the landscape. It begins, for example, with the ways of construction of stone walls and live hedges as field enclosures, it does not, however, stop with this interest. One looks further for the extent of particular kinds of field enclosure as elements of a landscape that was occupied and transformed by farmers at a past period of time. It is the extent and association of spatially arranged phenomena of the landscape that give the key to this approach.

Otto Schlüter in Germany wrote in 1906 that he desired a limitation of the subject matter and greater objectivity in the geography of Man. He suggested that it should aim at the form and spatial arrangement of earthbound phenomena as far as they are perceptible to the senses. This method, he claimed, should be morphological and its procedure parallel to the study of landforms. It should not stop at the classification of the phenomena of the landscape (be they fields, farms, field boundaries, urban houses, railroad tunnels, or telegraph poles), what Hartshorne called some 30 years after (1939) "the phenomenology of landscape." It should seek to determine associations of such phenomena in their spatial arrangement.

A similar trend was evident in France at the same time. In 1910 the work of Jean Brunhes on *La Géographie Humaine* was published. This work received widespread recognition among scholars and resulted in his appointment to a research chair in human geography at the *Collége de France* in 1912. Brunhes had the same objectives as Schlüter. He suggested that the study of the landscape in its spatial variations, and as the expression of occupance of human groups, is the autonomous field of geography, whereas ancillary fields are those which deal with matters "beyond the essential facts" of landscape. These latter embrace the distribution of population, the geography of work, the geography of political societies, and the geography of civilizations, where these are associated with the "essential facts" of the human habitat.

It is universally recognized on the continent today that the study of landscape as the areal variation of the earth's surface has had a profound impact on research over the past generation following the works of Schlüter and Brunhes. The concept was critically appraised by Carl Sauer in the United States in his *Morphology of Landscape,* published in 1925, in an effort to give focus to the field of geography in America. His views had a strong impact on a few younger scholars in the Middle Western Universities. Regretfully, it has to be recorded that the pursuit of its themes with a few conspicuous exceptions (noted below) has been abandoned in the post-war years. In Britain, the landscape concept made no impact whatever before World War II, as the present writer can testify by the cold reception given to his studies of urban morphology. Insistence on social processes is now helping incidentally in the understanding of landscape currently. What is persistently ignored is that the regional concept seeks to understand the modes of grouping of similar phenomena and the spatial interconnections of unlike phenomena that are symbiotically interrelated. This is the essence of the regional concept which begins and ends with the spatial variations of the world around. It still awaits clear and persistent dedication, whereas the current trend is to get involved (and sometimes lost in a *cul de sac*) in mathematical equations and social behavior, without regard to the forms and grouping of land, land use, and buildings of the human habitat.

Anglo-American criticism of the landscape concept in the late thirties was directed to the shortcomings of certain followers rather than to the views of the founders, whose works, let it be frankly stated, were just not adequately known. Brunhes and Schlüter demonstrated in substantial works, long after their early conceptual statements, just how they would put them into operation. Schlüter devoted his life to a study of the distribution and mapping of the forested and forest-free areas of central Europe at the beginning of the German tribal settlement around 500 A.D., published in the fifties. Brunhes, over 30 years ago, and with the collaboration of a younger man, Pierre Deffontaines, wrote a two-volume work on the geography of France in which his ideas, many of them well beyond "the essential facts," were developed.

There was a tendency in the thirties for Anglo-American writings (there was precious little quality research) to be merely descriptive, or, as someone called it, "cryptic." However, to condemn the inadequacies of weaker brethren is not fair pleading. The weakness of the Anglo-American approach was its failure to cope with the areal arrangement of the phenomena of landscape, and particularly to assess the historical origins and spread of particular patterns of distribution. Since 1945, there has finally emerged a stronger emphasis on the origins of the distribution and associations of spatial phenomena as regional entities, which the two founders had urged at the outset. A French geographer writes (in a private letter) for example, that today his colleagues are interested less in the classification of different varieties of *bocage* and *campagne,* (enclosed and open field landscapes), although such work is necessary as a starting point of investigation. They are today concentrating on the historical origins of particular patterns of distribution as associated phenomena in a changing rural landscape. The same holds good for field systems, rural settlements, and urban forms. The essential for the regional concept is not the origin of a new form, the mode of construction of a wall or of a house, but the distribution and association of these forms as integral parts of the changing humanized landscape. Today at last, the aim of Schlüter and Brunhes (probably without awareness of the fact) is being pursued under the title not of "morphography"; nor "morphology." It is now labelled "morphogenesis."

There is very little excuse for ignorance of the work of continental scholars over the past 50 years. I never so much as heard from the lips of my teachers the name of Otto Schlüter in the twenties. It is really amazing that Brunhes' scheme of classification of the "essential facts" of landscape, although available in English in 1920, had not the slightest impact, in either understanding or adoption, in Britain and America between the wars. I can testify to this again, since it was in this period that I served my apprenticeship. It is a matter of unceasing interest to the writer to speculate why this should be. It may be because Brunhes laid emphasis on classification of man-made phenomena (facts of unproductive occupation, facts of vegetable and animal conquest, and facts of destructive economy), although his work received immediate and signal recognition in France. It seems to this writer that the development of this concept was retarded by the great strength and persistence of the environmental approach (to which again I can testify personally), that began with "the physical base" and a thorough, and what was considered an indispensable, grounding in geology. There was thus a lack of direction in the evaluation of historical antecedents or contemporary dynamic processes. There is, however, considerable evidence in current researches of a readiness of some scholars to devote their energies to the origin and spread of cultural ingredients of the landscape. Such are American studies of the spread and distribution of the covered bridge, the layout of the county town, the assembly of the southern plantation, and of certain traditional types of houses. Particular mention should also be made of the work of Christopher Tunnard of Yale, professor of architecture, on the historical development and spread of urban forms in America. In Britain, certain economic historicans, bearing the title of "industrial archeologists," have made a big stir in recent years and have stolen a march in landscape study, although a few younger geographers are following after in their researches and publications.

5. THE ECOLOGICAL IMPACT

The further development of the Geddes' trilogy of Environment, Function and Organism in the study of human groups in their environmental settings is reflected in the ecological impact in the last 50 years. The mechanistic determinism of social Darwinism dies very hard and it was not, in effect, until this generation that the ecological approach made an extended impact.

The term ecology is derived from the Greek *oikos,* meaning a place to live in. It is concerned, in other words, with the scientific study of the habitat of lifeforms. The word was first used by the German biologist, Ernst Haeckel, in 1868. It was not until around 1900 that the study of lifeforms on the earth took shape, although the beginnings can be traced in the works of Humboldt. Schimper's German classic on plant geography appeared in 1898; the work of Warming, a Dane, in 1895; of F. E. Clements, an American, in 1905; and A. F. Tansley, a Britisher, in the 1920's. Animal ecology developed more slowly but has assumed prominence in recent years notably in terms of "the territorial imperative." An ecology of Man can hardly be said to have emerged as to objectives, concepts, and procedures until the twenties. Social scientists at Chicago, led by E. W. Burgess, and R. Park, cultivated the field. There was very little, if any, cross-fertilization, with the geographers across the way in Rosenwald Hall, who, under Harlan H. Barrows, were seeking to develop the same approach, and, incidentally, actively pursue to this day the same disciplinary goals.

The regional concept is concerned with the modes of spatial association of phenomena over the earth's surface. Its first task is to develop procedures of analysis, both quantitative and qualitative. This means procedures of analyzing and synthesizing spatial systems of earthbound phenomena, both as unique units, and as members of generic worldwide (or continental) systems. The elucidation of such associations, as was clearly shown in plant ecology at the end of the nineteenth century, involves three ecological determinants, that are the successors (in my view) to the earlier trilogy of Place, Work and Folk. These are: Site; Symbiosis; and Innovation.

Site, as in plant ecology, refers to an area that is homogeneous with respect to a particular distinctive set of associated physical conditions that are relevant to human occupance. The repetitive spatial arrangement of farmsteads or roads or the uses of land all show some degree of repetitive adjustment to a uniform site.

Symbiosis refers to spatial interconnections or interlinkage of places. It finds expression in the functions, size and spacing of settlements, and in the extent of man-made administrative divisions and state boundaries.

Innovation refers to the origins, direction of spread, and present distribution of items in a culture complex, such as the digging stick, the dog, maize and potatoes, modern technical aid in the form of farming techniques, diet, ploughs, latrines, radio, and capital investment. Such innovations do not, have not, and cannot, spread to all peoples in all areas. They follow certain directions and can be deliberately propagated with success only in certain acceptable contexts.

All this is what is meant by the ecological approach. It fixes squarely on the characterization of spatial groupings, not as a partial exploration in the framework of the physical environment, nor on the wider but still vague triad of Place, Work and Folk. This is the ecological approach to the regional concept. It is the key to the conceptual structure and purpose of this book.

6. THE QUANTITATIVE IMPACT

There has been a remarkable development in the past 20 years, since 1950, in the methods and procedures of measuring the modes of distribution and association of terrestrial phenomena—that is, of regionalization.

It must be emphasized, however, that the contemporary workers are building on the scaffolding erected by two German predecessors. August Lösch, an economist, who died in 1945 at the early age of 39, produced a definitive work in 1940 on *Die raümliche Ordnung der*

Wirtschaft. This was translated into English and published in the States in 1954 with the title *The Economics of Location.* Walter Christaller, a geographer (who died in 1969) received, for various reasons, tardy recognition by his colleagues in Germany, but has received signal attention in other countries. His major work, *Die Zentralen Orte in Süddeutschland: Eine ökonomisch - geographische Untersuchung über die Gesetzmässigkeit der Verbreitung und Entwicklung der Siedlungen mit städtischen Funktionen,* was published in 1933 and has recently appeared in the States in an English translation. (Constantin Doxiadis, a Greek, of Athens, Greece, who is an international figure in the realm of practical regional planning, gave lengthy acknowledgement to Christaller in a *Profile* in *The New Yorker* two or three years ago, in which he ascribed to this modest German scholar the basis of his conceptual framework of "ekistics" or, as Doxiadis explained it, "the scientific study of settlement.") These two German scholars found the roots of their thoughts among German predecessors. The determinants of agricultural spatial systems, for example, were investigated theoretically by J. H. von Thünen in a work published in 1826 (*Der Isolierte Staat in Beziehung auf Landwirtschaft und Nationalökonomie*), and J. G. Kohl, who studied under Carl Ritter in Berlin, published a work entitled *Der Verkehr und die Ansiedlung der Menschen in ihrer Abhängigkeit von der Gestaltung der Erdoberfläche* in 1841—with a second edition appearing approximately a hundred years later (1950). This recital gives sufficient indication of the stimulating progress in the study of regionalization during the last 20 years among geographers, economists, sociologists, mathematicians, and others.

From the research literature in English, special mention should be made of the proceedings of the Regional Science Association, under the direction of Walter Isard at the University of Pennsylvania. Isard is also the author of two books, *Location and Space Economy* (1956), and *Methods of Regional Analysis* (1966). Britain has produced Peter Haggett's very relevant work on *Locational Analysis in Human Geography* (1965) and a large symposium (the second) on *Models in Geography,* edited jointly with R. J. Chorley (1967). Isard and his colleagues are devotees of a distinct and important new field called "regional science," which means essentially the mathematical analysis of geographic variables of any kind. Haggett, much more appropriately to our theme (and herein lies the importance of his contribution), uses this new expertise in the study of the areal associations of individual phenomena among human societies over the surface of the earth. This is the central purpose of the regional concept. His contribution is paralleled by very recent continental researches. I note particularly, as a substantial exposition of these trends in France, a book by Paul Claval on *Régions, Nations, Grands Espaces* (1968). The above noted works are compendious volumes which it is not the purpose of this book to develop. The reader's attention is drawn to them as an essential part of the basic training in the regional concept.

Discussion will be limited here to those models and measures that are particularly relevant to the recognition and understanding of regionalization. For purposes of clarity of exposition, I follow closely the work of Peter Haggett on *Location Analysis in Human Geography,* London, 1965.

Spatial models are formulated in order to understand the nature of terrestrial spatial systems. Such models fall into several groups that are in the following three degrees of abstraction: properties at different scales; the representation of one property in terms of another; and the representation of properties by mathematical symbols. These three stages can be illustrated by reference to spatial systems from the surface of an area as revealed by an aerial photograph. This shows the real, not generalized, representation of the earth's features (Stage 1). The map, dependent on its scale, has some measure of generalization (grouping) of data by conventional symbols (Stage 2). Further generalizations from the latter, representing, for example, repetitive patterns of roads, fields, buildings, are represented by some kind of mathematical or symbolic expression (Stage 3). Thus, says Haggett—"Models then represent idealized parts of systems, just as systems represent an arbitrarily separated segment of the real world."

Models may begin with simple postulates and reach sophisticated conclusions. Von Thünen in 1826 in studying the disposition of uses of land, began by assuming a single city in a separate state with a flat uniform plain and one mode of transport by road (his work preceded the railroad). He found a tendency for uses to be arranged in concentric circles around the city as center, and that these uses changed with distance from the city, from which could be derived, in explanation of the uses (farmland, farm products, woodland, etc.), a simple rent gradient. This is, however, only one tendency, for other spatial determinants, such as soil variations and alternative markets to other city centers, complicate the spatial pattern. Yet he determined certain properties and determinants of the distribution and associations of economic phenomena.

Models may also be formed by simplifying generalizations, as in the study of route development. A published study of Ghana, for instance, begins with an empirical account of how the route pattern developed in space through time. From this pattern a series of successive phases is recognized beginning with coastal trading posts, and reaching currently a phase of interconnected linkages in a dendritic route pattern. Four stages are finally formalized and they are shown to be repeated in other developing countries.

Models may also be formed not by induction from observed data of repetitive spatial distribution, but by borrowing from related fields. My own modest effort in examining the geographic limits of Leeds in 1924 in the use of $1/2\ mv^2$ in fixing boundaries of equal accessibility by rail is an early example of this approach.

This whole trend should seek to strengthen the mainstream of geography as a single-focussed discipline with a scientific basis. This purpose is evidenced in two new major treatises by Jean Labasse, *L'Organisation de l'Espace; Éléments de géographie volontaire,* 1966, and Paul Claval, *Régions, Nations, Grands Espaces,* 1968. Labasse focusses his interpretation of the "organization of space" *(aménagement du territoire),* or, alternatively, with reference particularly to the domestic front, "environmental planning." He seeks not only to clarify the scope and purpose of this approach, but also to apply it to the solution of practical problems of human organization of space. Claval's work puts emphasis on the quantitative analysis of the areal distribution and association of economic phenomena. This follows the impetus from A. Lösch and W. Christaller, whose major works have just been noted. American and British geographers, as well as planners, such as Constantin Doxiadis, and "regional scientists," such as W. Isard in the United States, have awakened in the post-war years to the importance and opportunity for the application of such study to practical matters. Unfortunately, some assume, with evangelical zeal, that they are apostles of a "new geography," which, they claim, is far removed from what is often condescendingly described as "the traditional geography." Labasse and Claval formulate the purpose and principles of areal economic analysis within the traditional framework, and apply them to a more effective interpretation of regional associations of landscape and society over the earth. These associations Claval calls "regions, nations, and major world areas." Both these men use the techniques of quantitative areal analysis (and Labasse has done this admirably elsewhere in his monograph on the city region of Lyons) to help push forward geography in the mainstream of its heritage.

7. FIVE GENERATIONS OF GEOGRAPHERS

The regional concept has been particularly associated with geographers. We should, therefore, conclude with a brief biographical reference without burdening the reader with a list of names. The fact is that geography has been represented in Universities of Western Europe and the United States for about 100 years since the death of Ritter and Humboldt in 1859.

Starting then from this date, there have been five generations of geographers, many of whom were among the most distinguished and highly respected scholars of their period. They have been the outstanding exponents of the regional concept.

In Germany, there was a gap after the death of Ritter until exploration and teaching in the new universities opened new scholastic horizons. Chairs were established in the state universities of Prussia in the 1870's. The most distinguished leaders, acknowledged internationally by both anthropologists and geologists, were F. Ratzel and F. von Richthofen. A second generation were their students or followers. These included the founders of the subject as a university discipline —Vidal de la Blache in France at the University of Paris; Albrecht Penck in Vienna and Berlin; A. Hettner at Heidelberg; Otto Schlüter at Halle; J. Partsch at Breslau and Leipzig; H. J. Mackinder and A. J. Herbertson in the University of Oxford; W. M. Davis at Harvard (with whom should be associated the names of Mark Jefferson and R. de Courcy Ward); and Sten de Geer at Stockholm. The professional activity of these men covers broadly the last two decades of the nineteenth century and the first two decades of the twentieth century. During this period geography was fully established in many universities.

The third generation, which includes many distinguished names, contains the pupils of these men and students who were greatly influenced by them, or, in a few cases, others who entered the profession as self-trained geographers. This generation roughly fills the second quarter of this century and has its most active period in the twenties and thirties between the wars. Its leaders include: De Martonne, Demangeon, Baulig, and Blanchard in France; Hettner, Schlüter and Penck in Germany; Fleure, Roxby and Ogilvie in Britain; and Davis, Jefferson, Russell Smith and Bowman in the United States.

The fourth generation includes those who began their careers between the wars, have been leaders over the past 20 or 30 years, and are now reaching the end of their careers or are already in retirement.

A fifth generation includes those who have been trained since the last war and have been actively engaged in research and have 20 or 30 years of leadership before them. A sixth generation includes the young people who have recently launched their professional careers.

Each generation of scholars reflects the essentials of the philosophic approach of their age. Their leaders propagated new ideas that are pursued by their successors. All were actively concerned with strenuous and exacting periods of vigorous labor in the field, from the results of which emerged their major contributions to knowledge. Scholars of any category cannot be evaluated justifiably on the standards of the present. They must be evaluated in the light of the progress of philosophic and scientific trends which shift chronologically from one period to the next. There are periods of gradual change and periods of remarkable mutation. These leaders searched for new ideas and made contributions which transcended the traditional fabric in which they trained. Such is the march of knowledge; this is true of geography as of other fields.

8. THE WORK OF GEOGRAPHERS

Much of the work of these men was devoted in the last quarter of the nineteenth century, as a continuing and ever more specialized expertise to the present day, with the classification of particular sets of earthbound phenomena, and ways and means of mapping the data by countries, continents, and throughout the world. Indeed, many started their careers in some special field, especially in geology or biology and then later became "geographers" by their placement in new chairs in the universities. Their expertise and experience have been a most important contribution to knowledge that is all too often unknown or grossly undervaluated. Some of these scholars started their careers by mapping such data and then eventually reached out and sought human derivatives in what they called "geography." We are mindful of the earliest maps in the last decades of the nineteenth century. Many were published as wall maps of rainfall and temperatures, and winds and currents. The first classification of climates, the work of Herbertson on the atlas of meteorology, published in 1899, and his classification and mapping of the world's "natural regions" in 1905, were based on the superposition of various world maps. One is also mindful of the worldwide mapping of the distribution of population, types of economic activity and the like. Such contributions came a generation later than the preceding mapping of physical data, for it was not until the second quarter of this century that there emerged a clarity of purpose in classifying ecologically types of human groupings and their distribution.

Such work has continued over the last 50 years, based on the exact mapping of similar groupings or classes of phenomena that extend across and beyond the fixed boundaries of states and statistical units. Such contributions are too numerous to list; however, particularly important are the grouping of types of agricultural acitivity, levels of economic development, and forms of social structure or cultural realms. It is important to note that maps of this kind do not only cover the mapping of individual sets of phenomena for given statistical units (normally states). This is in large measure a routine cartographic exercise. More sophisticated procedures are involved in searching for similar spatial groupings as associations of individual spatially arranged phenomena. These are climatic regions, or types of agriculture. Concern is with groups of interrelated spatial phenomena, in their continental, and thus, potentially, their worldwide distribution.

Regional geography is normally regarded as the treatment of the variety of spatially distributed phenomena in a particular area, whether it is a local area, a country, or a continent. Spatially arranged data in the same area occur in sets of phenomena which are systematically (causally) interconnected (e.g., climate, terrains, vegetation, agriculture, urban associations). They occur together, however, with other sets of spatially arranged data that have no causal connection with each other. There is no necessary connection, for example, between erosion levels, and land use, an urban orbit, or dispersed farms. All of these are differentially arranged in any particular area. The problem for the regional geographer is to discover integrating processes that give some measure of identity and uniqueness to an area.

The mode of research, organization and presentation, has changed over the past 100 years (as we shall see in the next chapter) with changes in philosophic and scientific trends (holism, geographic determinism, ecological association, and quantitative analysis).

The last 50 years have witnessed a prodigious growth of knowledge and teaching of places and their variants over the earth in this general realm of enquiry. This is proven by the growth in the numbers of professors and students in the universities; by the great increase in the numbers of periodicals, published in about 40 languages throughout the world; and, above all, by the remarkable growth of the regular meetings of scholars from all parts of the world. An international organization has been in being for 100 years. Before World War I it was an assembly of scholars from many fields of earth study and was attended by numerous laymen. After World War I, when it was reorganized, it became the forum of professional geographers. At the meetings in London in 1964, there were nearly 2,000 participants and their sessions were opened by the Queen in the Albert Hall. The week's session of hundreds of papers was preceded and followed by prolonged *colloquia* and field excursions of some days duration by small groups in selected fields of research.

What have been the primary research interests of these scholars over the past 50 years and what relation do they have to the regional concept? These are questions discussed in my book on *The Makers of Modern Geography* (London, 1969). In summary the main trends are as follows:

1. There has been a continuous research interest in the forms of the land and in its areal variants, atmospheric and biotic. The study of problems of geomorphology has been an almost continuous concern of certain research commissions of the International Geographical Union. It has become increasingly active and specialized in western Europe over the past 25 years.
2. Study of human societies has received increasing attention, but often with a lack of clarity of problem, as to classification, distribution, or origin.
3. Increasing attention is now being given in two directions. One of these is the classification, mapping, and explanation of areal distributions with emphasis upon the origin and migration of hu-

man phenomena. The other trend is the pursuit of techniques of analysis; land use, morphogenesis, quantitative analysis and economic regionalization.

4. The one goal to which all of these trends contribute is the regional concept. This is concerned with the modes of arrangement and association of phenomena over the surface of the earth. The allegedly "traditional" approach as it is described in the United States and Britain is in disrepute, although this is a criticism of a concept that ceased to be pursued by continental scholars of stature a generation ago. The young exponents of a "new geography" are laudably, though somewhat belatedly, reframing their concepts, as has been done on many occasions by distinguished forebears of five professional generations. It is to an appraisal of the meaning of the regional concept as a distinct disciplinary field that these pages are dedicated.

PART II

THEORY

Chapter 4

REGIONAL UNITS AND REGIONAL SYSTEMS

1. THE MEANING OF THE REGIONAL CONCEPT

The term region is popularly used to refer to any geographical area that is adopted for the convenience of the user. In the scientific sense, however, it refers to an area in which all places have certain common characteristics by virtue of which it is distinct from the areas around. A "regional association" or, in other words, a spatial or geographic complex of phenomena, is an objective of research, not a point of departure. It seeks to evaluate the territorial factor in the life and organization of human communities. The main impetus to this concept came from the German geographer, Friedrich Ratzel, in the last two decades of the nineteenth century. He coined the concept of *Lebensraum,* one of the most challenging contributions to modern knowledge of human societies, although it has been much abused by geopolitics, especially in Nazi Germany, as an instrument of national policy. It reemerges in recent years among zoologists as the "territorial imperative." In current parlance, the regional concept studies spatial syndromes.

Several examples will clarify the concept in its fundamentals. A number of artifacts or habits may be distributed in such a way that their boundaries coincide. This is what American cultural anthropologists called years ago "a cultural area." A variety of agricultural phenomena, crops, rotations, size of holdings, products sold, may be located and then investigated as to their exact areal distribution. These phenomena may coincide in such a way as to permit the recognition of an agricultural association or complex. There are areas of community interest that may be measured, for example, by the circulation of newspapers or by the popular use of regional names. The structure of these different spatial complexes may be such that in some areas all the criteria are present. Borders and cores are, therefore, not necessarily sharply defined. Nodes are the focal points of these activities. Nets of roads and traffic flows are their channels of movement. Thus, regions are spatial or territorial complexes that consist of co-variant distributions of phenomena that are selected in order to discover and define a particular aspect of the totality of geographic space.

An association of areally arranged phenomena over the earth is based upon the distribution and coincidence of separate sets of areally arranged phenomena. These associations may be of physical configuration; of vegetation cover; of the works of man (farms, fields, routes and towns); of the density and arrangement of human populations; of one or more of the inherent characteristics of people (language, religion, family organization, economics or voting habits); of the movement of goods, persons, or ideas; and of modes of territorial organization. All these sets of phenomena are differentially distributed over the earth. They are distributed as continuities such as land use, relief, vegetation, as points (e.g. seats of mineral production, factories, villages, and towns), or as lines, as in the flows of traffic. They may be associated in such a way as to be bounded by sharp gradients of change, or they may be widely discordant so as to produce zones of transition in which regional associations are indeterminate.

The regional concept, as thus expressed, should be compared briefly with developments in the social sciences. For many years American sociologists have been discussing the scope and purpose of human ecology. The emphasis of the Chicago school some 40 years ago on the spatial aspects of community structure is referred to today as the "classical" period. This is reminiscent of the writings of Ptolemy and Strabo. It refers in this context to R. W. Park, E. W. Burgess, L. Wirth, and R. D. Mackenzie in Chicago. Amos Hawley, the sociologist, who makes this statement, asserts that the ecologist is concerned with the processes of human behavior. He explicitly relinquishes to the geographer the mapping of socio-economic data and the establishment of "natural areas," or functional areas as the geographer has preferred to call them for over 60 years. In the meantime, he continues, the human ecologist embraces human communities in relation to their habitat, by which he means the natural base, which he describes, as for plant communities, the *site-base.* This is without question a primary concern and responsibility of the geographer but it is only one of the aspects of regionalism, which embraces the areal variations of total human environment, both natural and man-made.

The community, as an areal grouping, according to O. D. Duncan, another American sociologist, contains four sets of elements: environment, population, organization, and technology. Ecologically, in any community there are interrelations (correlative or causal) between any two or more of these elements or their subdivisions. There are interconnections of such phenomena that are spatially coincident. The ecologist, Duncan goes on, envisages human communities as ecological complexes, and similar complexes are ecosystems. The terminology is sophisticated, using a vocabulary with many four-syllable words, but it is the same as the conceptual procedure formulated by Ritter and Humboldt. The fact is, however, that geographers have hitherto given maximum attention to spatial juxtaposition and boundaries and not so explicitly to the nature and interconnections of the various categories of spatially arranged facts and the social processes that lie behind them. They have also been swayed by the Land-Man equation instead of the search for territorial complexes. In current parlance, geography studies spatial systems. Its concern is not focused on individual distributions, but on their modes of spatial association, that is, with the territorial matrices that bind the individual ingredients together. Territory or land, I hasten to add, embraces both *site* or *terra firma,* and *location.* The latter was clearly stated by Strabo and most effectively developed by Friedrich Ratzel and is absolutely basic to the study of man's environment. The approach of the regional concept, as expounded in this book, is fundamentally ecological. It poses problems and seeks answers about the common spatial characteristics of human groups in their environmental settings.

2. REGIONAL PRESENTATION

Innumerable studies of the regional structure of small areas of some hundreds or thousands of square miles have been published over the past hundred years, and some comment is necessary on both the objectives and the methods of presentation of such studies.

One can clearly recognize several chronological changes, each of which reflects the changing philosophical and scientific trends, as summarized in the previous chapter.

In the first half of the nineteenth century research and presentation of the content of particular areas was mainly a matter of compilation of spatial data, presented without order and with little discrimination as to what information was relevant. This is generally referred to as the "holistic approach." The holistic approach is exemplified by the comprehensive works of Conrad Malte-Brun in France and Carl Ritter in Germany in the first decades of the nineteenth century. They are descriptive compilations of selected areas in the chorographic tradition of Strabo. Ritter sought to rise above what he called the 'mere description' of his contemporaries, in both the definition of the areas and the mode of selection and correlation of information. He was handicapped by the lack of data and wrote many volumes in collecting them to meet his final ends. E. Reclus wrote a second "universal geography" in the 1880's that still continued the same tradition, in spite of the rapid impact of the environmental approach. It should, of course, be noted that these works covered continental areas, that were virtually unknown and thus widely exposed to the play of fancy, with brief portrayal of their component parts, be they states, countries, or districts, however defined.

The environmental approach was predominent at the end of the century. It is exemplified by a study of a "fragment of England," in the southwest of Sussex by Hugh Robert Mill in 1900. This was a sample study of an area represented on the standard map of the Ordnance Survey on a scale of one inch to one mile. It was to serve as a model for descriptive monographs for each sheet for the whole country, much as monographs were published for the sheets of the

Geological Survey. The model was arranged as follows: geographical position: geological formations ("upon which are based the natural regions"); dangers to navigation off the coast; rivers, roads and railways; climate; woodland and agriculture; population (by parishes); and industries. The plan did not materialise, but a similar scheme was adopted by Mackinder, and developed later by Herbertson, his successor, at Oxford. This scheme was transmitted by students of Herbertson when appointed to the new departments of geography in the Universities. Students (the writer was one of them) were allotted a topographic sheet for "geographical description" in the form of a series of maps. This involved tracing of data direct from the topographic map, and possibly the preparation of other maps from statistical data of population by parishes. In other words, the area was descriptively fragmented and no effort or devices were demanded to synthesise or interpret the data, except in so far as they were coextensive with and dependent upon "the physical base." No wonder that geography became nothing more nor less than the study of terrestrial distributions for many. One began with the definition of the "natural regions," and then tried to fit human data into this framework. What did not fit was omitted.

Among the British geographers at this time, special mention should be made of the writings of P. M. Roxby. He wrote in 1913, with reference to East Anglia, that a natural region is "an area throughout which a particular set of conditions prevail, and *ceteris paribus*, a particular set of physical conditions will lead to a particular type of economic life. A physical unit tends to become an economic unit."

He expressed essentially the same view in an essay on the theory of natural regions in 1926. We should note, however, that this mature discussion of the regional concept, on an essentially humanistic foundation and in the Herbertson tradition, recognized that a unit area, may also be rendered homogeneous by human occupance. He also emphasised the role of "spatial relations" in the individuality of places, and recognized clearly, with the example of central Europe, the hierarchical mosaic of areas that make up the earth's surface. This thought, in which there is a strong environmental theme as a dominant concern, oriented research in the regional concept and presentation of its findings throughout the inter-war period.

The systematic approach became widely practiced in both field-based studies of small areas and in textbooks and other works from the 1880's until the 1930's. The conceptual framework was erected by F. von Richthofen in his inaugural address when assuming the chair of geography at the University of Leipzig in 1883. "Geography," he declared, "is the scientific study of the earth's surface, land, air, and water, plants, animals, and Man." The assembly and description of these variables in particular areal associations is called chorography in the strabonic tradition. Earthbound phenomena are to be studied with reference to their forms, substance, genesis, and dynamic (functional) interrelations. The growth of knowledge in these areas of enquiry (which at that time was rapidly developing) would eventually permit, and one should seek to promote, the explanation of these individual areal variables. This study he called chorology. This procedure was first accepted by the young Albrecht Penck in his book on *Das Deutsche Reich*, published in 1887, before he was 30 years old. In his later years, Penck rejected this approach, which he likened to a storied mansion, and sought a clearer focus in the areal variations of landscape and society. Alfred Hettner continued the Richthofen approach in his first field-based studies in Columbia and in his later comprehensive texts. We give two examples of the systematic approach, one by Hettner and the other in the large work on south Germany by Robert Gradmann. Both were German scholars of high distinction.

Alfred Hettner's monograph on the Cordillera of Bogota in Columbia was published in 1892 in the supplements to *Petermanns Mitteilungen*. Its arrangement may be summarised as follows:

1. Structure, surface relief, hydrography.
2. Climate.
3. Plants.
4. Animals.
5. Man—origin, spread and distribution.
6. Routes and trade.
7. Economic conditions.
8. Mode of life and cultural development.
9. Uniqueness of the Bogota Cordillera and its regional grouping.
10. The work contained four maps of geology, relief, places and distribution of population.

Gradmann's two volume work on *Süd-Deutschland* was published in 1931. It incorporated research essays on plant geography (his special field of expertise) and rural and urban settlements in Württemberg, that had been published in various sources for over 25 years. The chapters of the first volume, that deals with southern Germany as a whole, are as follows:

1. Land forms.
2. Climatic conditions.
3. Soils.
4. Plant and animal life.
5. Geographic development of settlement.
6. People and state in their areal development.
7. Race, speech, and folk.
8. Agriculture and rural settlement.
9. Forestry, hunting and fishing.
10. Towns and markets.
11. Industry and crafts.
12. Population distribution and density.
13. Trade and traffic.
14. Spiritual life.

The second (and much larger) volume contains chapters on 14 divisions of southern Germany. These are broad physical units and the treatment is patterned on the general topics for the whole of southern Germany in the first volume.

Essentially the same procedure has survived in more recent works published in Britain and America. Some of these reach high levels of scholarly competence. This is notably in the case of a book on Wales edited by E. G. Bowen, published in 1961. This is a collection of essays on a variety of spatial topics, ranging from peneplane surfaces to racial types and religious attitudes. Each topic is handled competently by the individual contributor with his own expertise, but simply, as Penck described it many years ago, as one story (or part thereof) of a mansion (without a staircase!). The only factor all have in common is Wales. This is arbitrarily prescribed by the editor, who presumably designed the structure of his edifice and the personnel of its builders. No wonder one so frequently asks the question in Britain "Whither regional geography?" The days of such systematic compilation masquerading under the title of "regional geography" are long since over. New trends of selection, orientation, and presentation began on the continent a generation ago, when many senior Anglo-American scholars were beginning their careers. Their students should have been alerted at that time to the new trends in the twenties by their teachers. Evidently, they were not, and scholarship continued in its ethnocentric seclusion. Writers of Anglo-American texts still present a thorough presentation of the physical elements, and add almost an addendum of human derivatives in the long outmoded environmental approach.

The ecological approach, in which land is interpreted from the standpoint of human occupance, has permeated a formidable body of research over the past 40 years, although almost exclusively in France and Germany. Special mention may be made of an exemplary and quite exhaustive work by Pierre Deffontaines on 'man and his works in the lands of the middle Garonne.' This work, prepared during the twenties, was published in 1932. It has made an indelible impression on the present writer for its creativity, perceptiveness, and original presentation. I have commented on this work in *The Makers of Modern Geography* as follows:

> 'The human effective' embraces types of habitation (the typology of individual buildings) and clustered settlements, from hamlets to towns, and their territorial framework (communes). The phases of settlement cover (a) depopulation in the nineteenth century; (b) overpopulation in the eighteenth century; (c) the recolonisation of the *bastides* (small new fortified towns) in the thirteenth and fourteenth centuries; and, (d) the demographic role of the Abbeys in the eleventh and twelfth centuries. Each of these receives one or more chapters. The *horizons de travail* are the dominant modes of occupation. Agricultural occupance begins with the systems prevalent today, and the sequence of treatment goes back to the "Wheat-maize cycle" of the seventeenth and eighteenth centuries, and the systems of cultivation in the middle ages. The industrial horizons of work embrace chapters on their present day character and distribution, and their character and locale in the eighteenth century. Commerce is examined in relation to the main transport arteries. of the great valleys and their adaptability to transport and the siting of trading sites (river regimes, flood plains, reclamation and utilization); the network of routes by river and road, and

modes of life associated with them. A last chapter is devoted to the market centers and their changing roles in the transport net.

This approach in pursuit of a diversity of selected problems, land use, urban impact on the country, and population trends, has characterised a long sequence of research monographs over the past 40 years.

It is appropriate to ask just how the approach of quantitative analysis contributes to the advancement of the regional concept. It seeks to formulate and apply general laws and systems of spatial distributions and to measure what is called "spatial interraction." It is not concerned with, and indeed in America explicitly rejects, the integrated study of spatially arranged phenomena in particular areas; unless, of course, statistical methods are applicable. The aims of its adherents are "nomothetic" and they disdain what is called the "ideographic" approach. Quantitative analysis provides new tools in spatial analysis, which the regionalist should undoubtedly master and use. It also provides many new stimuli to understanding the spatial distribution of social phenomena. Indeed, "regional science" has made its appeal mainly to social scientists. But it pays little attention to regional integration of land and people. There is not yet in print in America a single research study of any kind that purports to be an integrated regional study of a small area. Quantitative analysis is a tool in the study of both natural and social processes in space. Its impact presents a challenge, for quantitative techniques need to be applied to the furtherance of regional synthesis.

3. THE REGIONAL CELL

The landscape, be it in a big city or in the farmlands of the Middle West, is made up of a mosaic of *form units.* These are entities of associated landscape elements; that is, of relief, vegetation, land use, and settlement. Human groups in their various activities, economic, social, and political, are arranged in space as *functional units* that either correspond in their smallest detail to a single form unit or to an association of sections of several form units. Human societies are organized in a hierarchy of areas from these *spatial units* or cells, such as the farm (which is an operating unit of agricultural use), dwelling, or factory, to large spatial groupings of a social, economic, cultural, and political character. It is only in terms of these human functional groupings, the areas they cover, and how they operate as entities, that the character and areal interrelations of the elements of the landscape become understandable.

The study of the distribution and density of people and settlements demands thorough analysis of small localities as a means to understanding major characteristics and issues of Man's occupance of the Earth. The interpretation of such local patterns, when worked out on a large scale, rests on such considerations as the amount of land under cultivation, the character and intensity of Man's agricultural use of the land. Laws of inheritance, migratory movements of all kinds, the balance of birth and death rates, in their areal variations, are other factors in this equation. Then, again, one must consider the proportion and geographic distribution of the people who are engaged in industry, commerce, and administration, as well as in agriculture, mining or forestry. These are typically concentrated in central places (usually vaguely described as "towns"). They are however, also distributed widely over the countryside among the agricultural people, in ways and with frequencies, that vary from one areal context to another, and that depend on cultural character and historical change, as well as on present function. All these are aspects of the distribution of Man and his settlements on the face of the earth that are raised by the regional concept.

4. REGIONAL HIERARCHIES OF LANDSCAPE UNITS

The smallest entity of natural terrain may be only a few square miles in extent. It is a homogeneous complex of physical conditions, embracing altitude, degree of relief, bed-rock, soil, vegetation, and drainage. The smallest unit of the first order, may be a unit slope, such as a flat valley floor, a "steep" slope, a "flat" plateau surface, or a low flat strip between two valley floors (interfluve). Such a unit may be termed "a terrain facet." It has been defined by plant ecologists as a "site" or an "ecotope." (Alternative terms used among German scholars are physiotope and biotope.) A contiguous group of such varied but repetitive facets forms a composite geographic unit, that was called about 40 years ago a "stow" (from an old English word) by Unstead In Britain (1933), and a "chore" (from the Greek root meaning district) by Sölch (1924) in Germany. Such unit areas of the second order are locally repetitive in association with other similar units so as to form compact and contiguous groupings of a third order.

The latter may be called "tracts." They can be readily identified from maps on a scale of about 1:100,000 (one and a half miles to one inch). They in their turn can be grouped into larger homogeneous areas of a fourth order. These have a dimension suited to a scale of 1:500,000 (about eight miles to one inch). These units in turn are associated with others of the same order but of different character to cover a continental area, that may be called a province or realm of a fifth order. These units may be ultimately associated with climatic-vegetation realms or "biomes" of a sixth order throughout the world.

This kind of investigation has been especially notable in Germany over the past 20 years or so. I have personally undertaken (over a period of many years!) such an investigation in Germany. It was based on map study as well as on field observations on foot, by cycle, by car, and by plane.[1]

5. REGIONAL HIERARCHIES OF SOCIETAL UNITS

The patterns of the natural terrains are clearly reflected in the adjustments of human occupation and organization. It would be quite wrong, however, to assume (as was frequently the case a generation ago) that the latter can be determined adequately in terms of the terrain, and that human territorial groupings are limited to such adjustments. Human functional groupings must be examined *per se* in their areal texture in terms of human activity and in terms of the reflection of this activity in the man-made habitat.

A farmstead may lie in the midst of its own fields (a compact operating unit, with the farm located alone). It may be located in a place, clustered with other farmsteads, separated from its strips of land, that are scattered throughout the farmland of the village community. The latter operates over a defined geographic area and embraces the operating units of its cultivators. In this sense, it is a social, economic and political space-grouping. It is the center of a clearly defined area, gemeinde, gemeente, commune, parish. The size, shape, and population of this area vary widely, as does the mode of grouping of the farms and fields within it. The village is thus in some degree a functional unit. The compact peasant holding or the group of buildings with divided strips in one village (that for centuries was organized

[1]The maps will be found reproduced in my major work on *Germany: A General and Regional Geography*, Second edition, 1961.

in varying ways on a communal basis) may lie entirely within one type of landscape or may even include sections of several landscapes, or simply small facets of the same terrains, such as woodland, meadow, arable, or heath. Several sections of diverse facets would thus make up a functional (that is, an agricultural) operating unit, and a group of adjacent farms make up a communal village group.

The mode of farming of such a small community is repeated in neighboring communities so as to form an area with similar farming practices. These common practices are reflected in the character of the country landscape, or the modification of it to suit new practices in the use of the land, in the arrangement and disposition of operating units, and in the siting of farmsteads. Factories, non-rural homes, and services may occur in such a countryside, and their character, distribution, and interrelations must be localized and explained. A village community and its neighbors, for example, may be part of a spatial complex in which industry and agriculture are intermingled. The nature of such a complex is reflected in the character, locale, arrangement, and functional (symbiotic) interdependence of its elements. A more extensive space-grouping will have distinctive characteristics of language, traditions, and folklore. In other words, the village always forms the cell of a wider geographical circle of associations. The latter are economic, social and political in kind. They are physiological associations of society as opposed to physiognomic associations of the habitat or landscape.

This ecological interpretation of Man on the Earth may be carried much farther. The variety of production within one holding and among adjacent villages has been the basis for the local exchange of products and services in the self-sustaining economies of Europe and the Orient. These transactions are concentrated in places that assume a special character called "urban." One of the most important activities of the small country town is to organize the exchange and provide the services for the surrounding countryside. Such services are needed by people everywhere and must be readily available by road from a network of urban centers. The functions of these places in past periods, however, have not been limited to service. They also included crafts, defense, religion, and administration.

In the last hundred years, new techniques have caused an enormous massing of populations and activities on the site of raw materials and at rail, river and, sea-coast locations, where raw materials are unloaded and transformed for widespread distribution. Urban centers emerged in Western Europe primarily as service points in the widest sense in the middle ages and, over most of America during the past hundred years in the days of the horse and buggy. There was preserved in these centers a "human scale," of which Lewis Mumford writes. In the generation of the exclusive dominance of the railroad in the late nineteenth century, population amassed in small areas on or near coalfields; accumulated around pre-existing nodal points; or was dispersed on farms in the great continental interiors that had to lie within a road haul of some ten to 20 miles of a rail-head. Such was the spatial impact of the "civilizing rails." It was highly localized in centers and strips. In the last 50 years, the metalled highway and the electric power line have spread their net much more universally. Urban agglomerations, in America and western Europe particularly, have expanded and exploded. The dwellings of urban workers may reach extremes of 50 miles from their places of work. Areas for recreation are similarly within their daily reach. Motels cluster and sprawl at strategic sections of the great American highways. Land uses are being adjusted to new facilities of access. There is emerging a far-flung range of symbiotical relations that cuts right across the patterns of the physical landscape and of the human relationships and institutions that have been handed down from the past. Functional relations and organizations are in rapid process of territorial regrouping, from farm unit, commune or township, to city, metropolis, major regional entity, an inter-state association. Such is the changing hierarchy of functional entities, from farm to world.

We need to understand the spatial demands and trends of human groupings in order to advise on remedial adjustments in terms of human welfare and happiness. Remote residential subdivisions in Arizona, urban destruction in city cores, independence for small peoples living in isolation, just do not make sense and will be of no avail, unless they meet with certain minimum requirements of sociogeographic integration in the positive reconstruction of Man's environments. Such is the major problem of Man's occupance of territory, for there is currently a lack of concern or understanding of the spatial element in the life of Man as a social and sociable animal.

6. REGIONAL CONSCIOUSNESS AND NAMES

Regional consciousness means the awareness of togetherness among the people in an area. Their common attitudes reveal a close association from birth in an undisturbed milieu with either a distinct environment or a distinct sociogeographic group among the people who live in the same locality. In Britain, regional consciousness has often been obscured by the great shifts of population to the urban areas and the decline of social awareness among the country populations, where urban attitudes are making an increasing geographic impact. However, this should not be exaggerated, for many regional names survive in popular usage. Such are the Cotwolds, the Weald, Holderness and Craven. All of these are regional names that, as maps and records readily reveal, have been in use for centuries. The counties, as governmental units, descend from the middle ages and bear little relation today to the socioeconomic affinities that have emerged since the Industrial Revolution. They are often quite inadequate as units of modern public organization and service, yet they survive as a frame for many aspects of social life, not the least important of which is the national summer sport of cricket. In France, where most of the countryside has been subjected to little change by modern developments, there is an intimate association between the peasant and the terrain he cultivates, the woods he uses for fuel, and the pastures for his livestock. The speech of peasantry abounds in evidence of such "perception of environment." Terrains are designated not by the fancy names of the geologist or pedologist, but by simple terms which reveal their utility and special attributes and problems for agricultural use by the peasant. Regional names are also used for particular and more broadly defined landscapes. *Montagne,* for example, is used in the Central Massif of France not for high and rugged relief, but for land that is used for summer pasture, wherever it may be, on or off the farm holding. *Côte, vallée, plaine, terre chaude* and *terre froide,* etc., are used with such local connotations. Again, the associations of people in a district are often recognizable by regional names. These are often recorded on ancient maps, and even go back in extent and name to the days of the Roman occupation. In many cases, of course, the geographic connotation (the area to which the name refers, and indeed the meaning of the name) have changed through time with changes in life and organization and use of the land. Attention to such local district names *(pays)* has been given in innumerable studies in the geographic research literature of France for over 50 years.

Of particular significance among the functional groupings of society are those revealed by "names on the land," as they have been described in America by George Stewart. With origins often wrapped in obscurity, such areas do not betoken necessarily a type of country, but an area that for some reason or other was regarded, and often still is regarded in popular usage, as a distinct area. Among the oldest and the best known are the names of physical areas, especially where clearly marked off from their surroundings. Such are the Vosges, Black Forest, Harz, Rhön, and, Vogelsberg in Germany. The Ozarks or the Flint Hills are examples in America. Many smaller and less well known countrysides have such distinctive names.

These names and the areas to which they apply are not as simple as may be assumed at first thought. One may ask, for instance, what is the extent of Harz or Vosges as a geographical name? Where are the limits and what meaning is associated with them? There is, for instance, a High Vosges and a Low Vosges, an Upper (Ober) and a Lower (Unter) Harz. In Britain one may ask, what are the limits of the Cotswolds or Weald? In America, what are the locale and limits of the Middle West, the Deep South, New England, the Blue Grass Region, the Great American desert, the Flint Hills, and the Ozarks? The answers to these questions must be sought in old maps and documents as well as in popular usage, past and present.

Many of these district names in Europe have their origins in the remote past and have figured on maps and in popular usage for centuries. They are the names of areas associated with human groups who have felt a "togetherness" in attitudes, origins, associations, and organization. This has long been referred to in Britain as "regional consciousness," though few attempts have been made to measure it. As noted above, such units cover the land of France. The small units are known as *pays* (a word derived from the Latin *pagus*, a Roman unit area which survives in later human groupings). Examples are the *pays* of Beauce and Brie south and east of Paris. Both of these are old popular and cartographic names; and they are coterminous in popular usage with distinct kinds of landscape. Larger units (such as Brittany and Burgundy) were for centuries (down to 1789) the main areas of regional government in France and have a strong feeling and tradition of regional consciousness. They are generally referred to as the *histori-*

cal provinces. Exactly the same features are found in the German lands, where the name *gau* has the same etymological root and has the same geographical meaning as the French *pays,* both being derived from Latin *pagus.* The following are some of the commonest names in France, indicating close association with a town: Orleans, Orleannais; Angers, Anjou; Macon, Maconnais; Soissons, Soissonnais, etc. Many of these names and their areas have persisted with central cores for a thousand years. Their boundaries were always vaguely defined since there were no accurate maps, for which reason physical features easily recognized on the ground, such as rivers and ridges, were often taken as arbitrary limits.

Early administrative and ecclesiastical units, such as bishops' dioceses, the secular areas of lords and counts, and indeed the tiny cells of village organization, were based on preceding Gallic divisions. The Roman *civitates* were followed by the Merovingian and Carolingian divisions in Gaul and the Rhinelands. Further east, in "inner Germany," these divisions were based on the areas occupied by the distinct German tribes *(Volksgemeinschaften).* In spite of the bewildering complexity of the political map of Germany down to the opening of the nineteenth century (and the persistence of many of its anomalies to our day), many of these district names have persisted for a thousand years, sometimes as existing political or ecclesiastical areas, sometimes as popular names. They cut across the arbitrary bounds of the rags and tatters of land that emerged during the period of feudal disintegration in the later Middle Ages.

The major historical provinces in Germany, many of which were liquidated around 1800, are the equivalents of the French provinces. They are often called the *historische Landschaften.* The latter term means something in German that is entirely different from the literal meaning in English. It designates a unit of organization and life of human society. Many of these major areas, their cores and indeed, their traditional boundaries, correspond with the old tribal duchies. Such are Swabia, Franconia, Old Bavaria, and Lower Saxony. Others have names and bounds derived from medieval political units within which geographic framework the life and organization of the people developed and functioned for centuries. Examples are the old dukedoms of Berg and Mark in the Rhine Plateau, east of the Rhine; Baar, Klettgau and Hegau in southwestern Germany between the southern end of the Black Forest and the Swabian Jura and the shores of Lake

Constance. Further examples are the Kraichgau, the open (woodless) and fertile limestone country between the Black Forest and the Odenwald, and the Bergstrasse, the fertile strip at the foot of the Odenwald in the Upper Rhine Valley. It will be noted that many of these local districts bear the suffix *gau*, to which attention has already been drawn. These are the names given to the earliest districts into which the German tribal groups segregated. They are usually found to have had at the time of their emergence in the first millenium A. D. (500-800 A.D.) a fertile and closely settled core and a surrounding border of forests or mountains that for centuries often served as natural boundaries and preserved the individuality of the area in spite of its subsequent political disintegration. Such entities retain today distinct characteristics of dialect, dress, speech, folklore, and architecture. One city often served as an effective common bond, and sometimes the whole may have been held together by its persistence as a political unit, resisting in the past the disintegration that occurred elsewhere. Germany, like France, is rich in such geographic functional entities, and the origin of the names and the areas to which they apply is of special significance in the search for the relations of human groups, in the past and in the present, to their habitat.

One of the most explosive and challenging of regional names is *Deutschland.* This has long figured on old maps. It is the expression of a regional awareness, although its meaning and limits defy description. It referred in the past to the extent of the Reich which for a thousand years was a congerie of political territories until its liquidation at the beginning of the nineteenth century. It has also had an obscure, but real, cultural connotation that has been explored by cultural historians, social anthropologists, and others. The growth of nationalism had political overtones. This is evident in the words of the anthem written in 1848, that in 1871 became the national anthem of the new *Reich,* although its claims far outreached the frontiers of the new Reich. Alsace (France) and the southern Tyrol (Italy) are among its transitional borderlands. The name became involved in the political concept of Mitteleuropa between 1871 and 1918. It was revived with an active political connotation by Hitler in the thirties. The current trends of European affairs, as evidenced by the Common Market, is a continuing manifestation of the same phenomenon. The name has thus a historical, a cultural, an economic, and a political connotation, with which interstate affairs must establish a harmonious relationship for a lasting peace.

7. SYSTEMS OF WORLD REGIONS

A system is a series of phenomena that are interconnected by a common process. A regional system is a series of interconnected places, that are alike in character, or unlike but symbiotically interdependent in their functions and organization. A spatial association of this kind when envisaged on a worldwide scale as its universe of reference may be arrived at deductively or inductively. Regional systems are classified in terms of distinct criteria, located as to extent, and explained in regard to their common characteristics and location.

The deductive procedure starts with a worldwide frame of reference; chooses a particular set of phenomena with a known or supposed spatially differentiated distribution; collects relevant data throughout the world at particular places; classifies the data into particular categories; and devises ways and means of putting them on a map. No additional data are available for small areas, nor are the data uniformly distributed. The distributions are derived from a worldwide frame of reference and certain broad generalizations are made in locating areas and drawing boundaries around them.

The inductive approach works in exactly the opposite way. It seeks by a much longer and laborious process to determine in particular localities the cells of the mosaic of spaces, and builds outward from them until a country or continental or worldwide regional classification is reached. This was precisely the procedure followed in our researches into the mosaic of regions in Germany as noted on the previous pages. The two approaches are both valid, but they raise different problems and bring forward differing results. Those based on the inductive approach are much more reliable than the deductive approach, since the latter is based on a limited number of data, which are very unevenly distributed over the earth's surface. Therefore, in mapping the data the researcher must indulge in much intelligent guesswork, and make many assumptions about the situation at particular places and in unknown voids in order to bring them all to some kind of common denominator.

The expert energies of many scholars have been dedicated to the mapping of worldwide terrestrial distributions. This was mainly on a deductive basis, working from a very uneven and scattered collection of data of places. This was eminently true of major contributions at the end of the nineteenth century, such as the first mapping of the world's climates and the classic work of Schimper on vegetation. I do not refer to systematic studies of vulcanology, climate, oceanography, anthropology, and the like, but to the classification and division of the world, much of it by rather crude but scientific deduction, into areas, each of which has certain common characteristics based on certain selected criteria.

We may now turn to the concept of the natural region, that dominated the regional concept in the first quarter of this century. This concept was first clearly expressed in France, notably by Lucien Gallois, a geographer, in 1907. It was based on an investigation of the distinctive territorial entities in northern France. Two kinds were recognized. The first are entities of human life and organization. These find in certain areas (not everywhere) conscious and popular recognition among the people and have persisted (often with varying meaning) through centuries since the days of the Roman occupation. These entities are suggested by *nom de pays*, regional names, that may be revealed by popular contemporary usage, written records, and old maps. The second entities are associations of physical phenomena, which might be detected by field observation, or, as was made possible in the late nineteenth century, by large scale topographic and geological mapping. At this large topographic scale, an area within a day's journey, such entities are mainly based on uniformity of relief: soil and geological structure, with which there tend to be associated distinctive groupings of vegetation, soil, and climatic variations. These entities were described as "natural regions." Gallois noted that there was a tendency for the two kinds of entities frequently to correspond with each other. However, he also noted that this was only one tendency, for many human entities, especially if focussed, for example, on a town, tended to overlap and combine sections of two or more contrasted natural entities. There was no determinism in Gallois' approach, although there emerged an almost automatic tendency among contemporaries at this time to assume that the natural entity tended to have a uniform set of human activities and conditions. It should be noted that Gallois limited his observations to the north of France and made no wide and sweeping genralizations. His concepts were sound. The assumptions made by his followers were not, for they were all too frequently based on the deterministic Land-Man approach of the period. But this mode of thinking and interpretation of small areas dominated work at the beginning of this century, especially in Britain and America, by the transference of the environmental mode of thought to the framework of the regional concept. The "region" was a goal of investigation for Gallois. For the vast majority, to our own day, it is fallaciously treated as a convenient vehicle for some kind of presentation.

The regional concept was developed around 1900 with reference to the division of the world into systems of major entities. The first two such systems were presented by A. J. Herbertson in Britain in 1905 and A. Hettner in Germany in 1908. In each case the principles were entirely different, the one producing a system of *generic* regions, and the other a system of *specific* regions, although both aimed at a world wide classification of homogeneous entities.

Herbertson used the term "natural region" to describe physical environments that were "inherent and not arbitrarily imposed." Indeed in a second statement in 1913 he defined them as "major regions" and dropped the adjective. The "regions" are defined strictly on a natural (physical) basis as a framework for the evaluation of human occupance, that may, of course, take on fundamentally different characteristics in the same kind of region in different parts of the world.

The task of regional delimitation, according to Herbertson,[2] involved two main problems: first, what criteria should be used in their delimitation; and second, how are the different orders of natural regions to be determined.

World maps were prepared under Herbertson at the School of Geography in Oxford, to show structural units, thermal belts, distribution of rainfall, and, vegetation. These were published as the Oxford Wall Map Series. From these distributions, and essentially those of climatic limits, Herbertson devised a classification which as P. M. Roxby claimed in the twenties, "whatever criticisms be directed upon it, represents one of the most fruitful and constructive achievements in the development of modern geography."

The world is divided into thermal belts (following A. Supan). Maintaining the Aristotelian astronomical terms, these are defined as follows: Polar, with no month with a temperature over 50° F; Cool

[2] A. J. Herbertson, "The Major Natural Regions of the World," *Geography*, Vol. 26, 1905. A whole number of *Geography* (Vol. 50, 1965) is devoted to the life and work of Herbertson.

Temperate, roughly between latitude 40° north and south, and the polar circles; Warm Temperate, approximately between 30° and 40°; and the Hot Belt with temperatures over 68° F most of all the year. The subdivisions of each of these belts are based mainly on rainfall and partly on relief. The classification is as follows:

1. Polar Regions:
   (a) Lowlands (Tundra)
   (b) Highlands or Ice Caps (Greenland).
2. Cool Temperate Regions:
   (a) Western Margin of West European Type.
   (b) Eastern Margin of St. Lawrence Type.
   (c) Interior Lowlands of Siberian Type.
   (d) Interior Highlands of Altai Type.
3. Warm Temperate Regions:
   (a) Western Margin or Mediterranean Type.
   (b) Eastern Margin with Summer Rains or China Type.
   (c) Interior Lowlands or Turan Type.
   (d) Plateau or Iran Type.
4. Hot Regions - Tropical:
   (a) Western Desert or Sahara Type.
   (b) Monsoon Summer Rain Type.
   (c) Summer.
5. Lofty Tropical or Sub-Tropical Mountains:
   Tibetan Type.
6. Equatorial:
   Wet Equatorial Lowland or Amazon Type.

Herbertson realized the existence of minor regions of varying orders, "organs, tissues, and cells" within the "macro-organism of the earth," however, at that stage, he asserted, definitions could not be attempted.

Herbertson's scheme has long provided a teaching medium in the high schools of Britain. It is, in fact, essentially based on climate. The lesser divisions reflect (or are assumed to reflect, where often in fact they do not) similarities of vegetation and relief. In all these respects Köppen's classification of climates, that is essentially based on the requirements of plant growth, was a sounder, though more complicated, framework. Herbertson's regions are almost identical with the later classification of climates by V. C. Finch and G. Trewartha in America (that are based on the Köppen classification), and of the *Landschaftgürtel* of Siegfried Passarge in Germany.

Alfred Hettner of Heidelberg published a series of articles in the *Geographische Zeitschrift* in 1908 on the "Division of Lands," and put forward a scheme on an entirely different basis.[3] He, like Herbertson, recognized regions of varying orders of scale *(Landschaften, Länder,* and *Erdteile).* Hettner, working down from the largest land units, first makes the distinction between land and water. Each continent is subdivided on the basis of physical and human characteristics. The procedure first appears in a book on Europe, published in 1907, and in a new edition in 1924.[4] The following major divisions are recognized: Northern Islands, British Isles; Scandinavian peninsula; Finland; France; Central Europe (meaning the Germanic lands, embracing the Low Countries, Switzerland, Bohemia and western Poland); East European Lowland; Spanish peninsula; Italy; Balkan peninsula; and, Greece. These divisions are not consistently marked out on the basis of physical conditions of orientation and configuaration. Human, as well as physical similarities, are assessed and consequently the criteria of definition are not consistent. Each of these major units is again broken down into smaller component parts called *Landschaften.* These, says Hettner, are usually, though not always, "tectonic-morphological units."

These comments serve to illustrate Hettner's conception of land units and the methods of their delimitation. It differs fundamentally from that of Herbertson. Herbertson devised a worldwide generic system based exclusively on consideration of natural, that is, physical criteria of climate and vegetation. On this basis a system of regions was worked out and mapped as a framework for the evaluation of human activities. It was the culmination in the regional concept of the Darwinian evolutionary interpretation of human affairs on the background of the natural environment. Hettner devised a system of land units on an inductive basis and considered both physical and human criteria in the recognition of territorial uniqueness. He also demonstrated clearly how each of these divisions may be broken down into smaller component homogeneous divisions. The inductive pro-

[3]A. Hettner, "Natürliche Einteilung der Erdoberfläche, *"Geog. Zeit.,* 1908; also *Die Geographie,* (1927), p. 293, and *Vergleichende Erdkunde,* Band IV, 1935, p. 338.

[4]A. Hettner, *Grundzüge der Länderkunde, Band 1, Europa,* 1st ed. 1907, 2nd ed. (rewritten), 1924.

cedure from the small locality to the world wide assessment of territorial associations is the chorological approach that lies behind Hettner's concept of "comparative regional geography." It is strictly in line with the concepts of Carl Ritter and his contemporaries.

A much greater fund of data, tied to places of occurrence, has characterized research on these lines over the past 50 years. This is based not only on a change of objectives and revised ways of using old data, but also on the enormous addition of new data, both physical and human. The geophysical year, for instance, added richly to the knowledge of places on the earth's surface on land and sea. States and international authorities have produced masses of census data for states and their subdivisions. Cultural anthropologists, geographers and others have undertaken exhaustive studies at first-hand of lands and peoples in many areas throughout the world. This information about places permits much more thorough portrayal and examination of the regional variations of human conditions throughout the world; economic and social structures, levels of living, racial types, cultural areas, etc. Such data can be used, when so portrayed, as bases for understanding and action.

Although such world systems are now pursued with sharply defined objectives and sophisticated techniques, both statistical and cartographic, they seek essentially the same goals as the pioneer works of Herbertson and Hettner two generations ago.

Chapter 5

MAPS AND MODELS

The scientific study of the territorial structure of human groups in their environmental settings demands a high proficiency in several skills. These are not to be acquired merely as courses of instruction but through diligent and unabated application. There is, moreover, in the long run, little distinction between scientific and artistic mastery. A musician or a craftsman devotes a lifetime to the perfection of his skills, and never reaches personal satisfaction. The same is true of any field of scientific endeavor. It is equally true of the field of enquiry of the regional concept in all its ramifications.

The special skills in question are: cartographic, statistical, documentary, and field observation.

1. THE MAP

Maps fall, according to their scale, into three orders, which may be called topographic, chorographic, and geographic. These differ in their characteristics and problems from the standpoint of both maker and user. The topographic map is the closest to reality, with scales larger than about one inch to one mile, including large scale "cadastral" maps on which all ground data can be reproduced exactly to scale. Maps on these scales demand some generalization (e.g., buildings and road widths are conventional) but the area represented is within contact and vision of a worker in the field. The second type covers wider areas, that may embrace a country or a continent, on a much smaller scale. These maps embrace the areas covered by hundreds of topographic maps. They therefore demand, by the limitations of scale, generalizations of a few categories in order to reach legibility of cartographic representation. The third type covers the whole world or a major part of it. It covers with ever greater generalization of categories the data that are shown on maps of a chorographic scale.

A map may be based on a ground survey, or on photography from airplane or earth satellite. Such procedures require one to classify, locate, and explain the variable cover of the earth's surface. One also needs to collate and record data personally on maps from a local scale to a worldwide coverage. This involves collecting innumerable place data (e.g., temperatures, population densities, crop production), and finding ways and means of putting them in the right locations on a map.

This is a vast field that puts exacting demands on training and competence. I subscribe to the following statement by B. J. Garnier in *Practical Work in Geography,* London, 1963, p. 77:

> "The importance of maps in geography arises from the subjects' fundamental nature. The geographer's laboratory is the world around him. Unlike the chemist, or botanist, or zoologist, however, he cannot bring his material into a room and examine it microscopically. Instead, the geographer must, as it were, reverse the telescope so as to see the world at large in miniature. A bug crawling over a rug can see only the immediate thread and has little comprehension of the whole pattern. Similarly, geographers, with their eyes, can see only the details around them. To appreciate the pattern and arrangement of these details it is necessary to draw a map, which is a way of reducing the material to manageable proportions."

I agree again on the basis of 40 years of experience and experiment, with the same author as he further comments as follows:

> "The geographical interpretation of maps is a vast subject which can only be considered briefly in a small book. Its importance in

the training of geographers is indicated by the prominent part it plays in most schools and university courses in Britain. It forms the core of practical work in most institutions, and some examinations, at both school and university levels, make it compulsory for a candidate to pass in this aspect of geography; if he is to pass in the subject as a whole. Particular care must be taken, therefore, to see that map interpretation is treated on lines which are both scientifically sound and in keeping with the aims of geographical work." (*ibid,* p. 90).

It is not necessary to discuss in detail what "map interpretation" involves. It is sufficient to say that it covers two main aspects, first, the preparation of maps showing the distribution of spatially distributed phenomena; and, second, the geographic description and interpretation of the topographic map, which, dependent on its scale, seeks to represent the phenomena of the earth, the land, its vegetation (natural and man-made) and its cover of roads and settlements.

Such study requires sophisticated techniques, as, for example, the interpretation of the relief of an area from its contours, or the repetitive aspects and distribution of road-nets, farms, villages, and towns. The description of an area as revealed on a topographic map is a special skill that seeks to portray the differential associations of phenomena of landscape. A clear and vivid summation (without explanation or theory as to origins of any single set of phenomena) of an area from a topographic map is, in this writer's judgment, the crucial test of the geographer's craft. It takes much repetition and experience to attain anything like perfection.

The preparation of maps, at the local or world level, involves the collation of data about places, for continental areas and, if possible through additional data or by intelligent guesswork, for the world as a whole. Data have to be grouped into categories and then appropriate concepts and techniques devised to put the data on maps. Data are collected by field observations on land and sea of winds, temperatures, barometric pressure, altitude, forms of the land, people (ethnic and demographic characteristics, group attitudes), farms, villages, towns, and products. They are needed as the essential basis for understanding the great spatial variations of lands and peoples in every area of the earth. Such collections embrace not only the popular atlases for general use, but also atlases that cover states, or sections of states, as records of resources upon which land improvement and social welfare can be rationally based. Such maps need generalized methods of representation. This requires the interpolation of lines between places for which specific data are available, and drawn on the assumption that there is a steady change of the relevant condition from one place to another. Examples are: contours (altitude), isobars (pressure), isotherms (temperature), isohyets (rainfall), and lines to enclose areas with the same densities of population and the same kinds of economic production. The data need to be grouped in combinations that reveal similar generic types of agriculture; of relief; of population density; of levels of economic development; of climate; and, of vegetation. Worldwide classifications and maps of this kind, by continents or for the world, reveal regional variations of phenomena over the earth. The recognition and mapping of these variations is an essential item in the craft of the geographer.

Such maps were published a generation ago to show particular categories of data such as: temperature, rainfall, products, density of population, etc. In recent decades, research has been directed to the grouping of interdependent phenomena into a small number of categories of spatially variable types. Examples are classifications of climates; of vegetation; of economies; of agricultural systems; of levels of economic development; of the density of population; of degrees of accessibility; of human cultures; of race types; of domesticated plants and animals; of political structures and their geographic range, both within and across the boundaries of states.

2. THE FIELD

A second skill is concerned with field observation of the variations of phenomena over the earth. Many great scholars in the past hundred years, especially in Germany, have been indomitable explorers in remote and unknown areas. On foot or horseback, or some kind of wheeled vehicle (culminating in our day in the jeep), they have traversed unknown and unmapped lands. They made arduous journeys on virgin trails, along which they selected, observed, and recorded, by note and sketch, the phenomena observed and the precise location of their occurrence. This task is relatively easy in countries which have detailed large scale topographic maps, as Western Europe. However, imagine the difficulties of recording in the field when traversing hundreds of miles in country for which only the crudest maps are available. Within the range of clear vision, what does one systematically observe day by day? How does one locate on a crude map what one observes? What symbols is one to use and how must one generalize? How is one to classify the data one records, for one is on a cross-country traverse, and it is unlikely that the same route can be crossed again, and others must be able to use the field records. These are questions that demand skilled procedures.

Field observation, then, is the beginning of any regional enquiry. It involves methods of classifying and recording by note, sketch, or map, the data of landscape and occupance. Let it be stated immediately that the problems thus presented vary tremendously with the scale of operation. The smallest distance that can be measured with the naked eye (on a diagonal scale) is about 1/100th of an inch. This is the diameter of a minute dot or a very fine line, and such accuracy of notation is not at all practical for rough recording in the field. Taking this, however, as a measure of limitation, on a scale of 1:25,000 (one inch representing roughly 2,000 feet), 1/100th of an inch would represent 20 feet; a scale of 1:250,000 (10 times smaller); 200 feet; and 1:1,000,000 (still 4 times smaller than 1:250,000), 800 feet. In other words, at smaller scales, individual phenomena, such as fields, roads, farms, villages, vegetation, and, hills, cannot be shown to correct scale. They must be generalized both as to their size and the extent of their occurrence. Problems of purpose and method are thus set by scale. The observation of phenomena in space as seen from a jeep or mule; traversing a rough trail for weeks on end across little known territory, or with a very inaccurate map, blown up, let us say, from a scale of 1:1,000,000 (one inch representing a little under 16 miles), is a very different proposition from studying any aspect of the landscape in thoroughly mapped countries such as Britain with a standard map of, say, six inches to one mile, or Germany with 1:-25,000, or even lesser scales, such as 1:63,360 or even 1:100,000.

This whole matter demands training involving (1) standards of basic observation; (2) clarity of objective, that conditions selection from the multiplicity of spatially differentiated phenomena; and (3) methods of representation in the field. It also could be that some kind of survey will have to be undertaken on a traverse, or in writing, as a diary of daily (and even hourly distance) intervals, to permit accuracy of location of the classified phenomena observed. Workers in remote areas have even been obliged to survey and produce maps of relief and surface cover of areas hitherto little known.

Several examples will serve to illustrate the procedure. Mapping the uses of land is a standard enquiry, of which there are innumerable examples. The best known case is that of the Land Utilization Survey of Britain. This is a series of maps on a scale of one inch to one mile (second edition, in course of publication, 1:25,000 or 2-1/2 inches to one mile) that cover the whole of Great Britain. These colored maps are a generalized reduction of initial field records prepared field by field on a scale of six inches to one mile. Land use was plotted by letter in the following categories: forest and woodland in various sub-categories; meadowland and permanent grass; arable (including rotation grass and fallow, and market gardens); heathland, moorland, commons and hill pasture; gardens, allotments, and nurseries; unproductive land; and ponds, lakes and reservoirs. A variant of this classification is being used by the Commission on World Land Use Survey of the International Geographical Union. We shall return to this theme in Chapter 7.

A further method of field mapping seeks to find the unit areas in which phenomena of land use are associated (whereas the previous methods use existing divisions), usually field by field (or groups of fields) as the unit of record. The "fractional notation system," as used originally in the T.V.A. land survey, involves a digital statement. A small area of recognizable uniform characteristics is selected. Its features are listed from a detailed table for reference to a short fraction for recording. The latter contains a denominator showing by numbers the physical characteristics (slope, drainage, erosion, stoniness, rock exposure, soil depth, soil fertility), each listed in a standard order with up to five categories in each. The numerator of the fraction indicates by several digits the major kind of land use (nine sub-categories), agricultural emphasis (14), field size (four), amount of idle land (four), quality of farmsteads (five). This long fraction is followed by a short fraction, which is a summary assessment, in which the numerator indicates (by one of five digits) the quality of the land use, and the denominator the quality of the physical conditions.

This system is capable of adaptation to a wide variety of purposes. Its main difficulty lies at the outset in the subjective assessment in the field of a land entity visible in the landscape. The best procedure in the case of agricultural use is to assess this unity in terms of physical conditions. Many of these conditions depend upon each other. Variants can be used in the demarcation of physical land-units, and their associated uses. This digit method can also be adapted to field recording of urban land uses in a city.

Two quite different procedures and problems may be instanced. An area may be covered with a variety of size and disposition of cultivated strips, such as is widespread in much of Western Europe. An exhaustive study of the Grande Limagne of central France (near Clermont Ferrand) mapped all the strips in the area. These were photo graphically reduced without generalization to a manageable scale. Spatial variants were discovered and the modes of origin and spread related to the impact of changing social and economic conditions affecting the settlement of widely contrasted physical conditions of the land.

A further use of the same method was the search for spatial variables of farm types in a small area in England undertaken as a part of the training of a group of undergraduates under the writer's direction. The primary criteria were the disposition of farm buildings and living quarters in relation to the type of economy. Several kinds of repetitive arrangements were found. These were then mapped and correlations were examined with the permanent (and changing) systems of rural economy. Building materials and traditions were also involved. The French geographer, A. Demangeon, was similarly interested in the thirties in the structure of farmsteads and their distribution. He finally undertook, with the aid of the Rockefeller Foundation, a nationwide survey of farmsteads, by sending a standard *pro forma* to a knowledgeable person in practically every commune in France. These data were finally mapped out for the whole country and were found to have marked localization, which then set the problem of explanation.

It will be clear that the classification and recording of spatially variable phenomena, both alone and in association with others, must serve not only as a personal source of reference but also as a legible source for other workers. This demands training in a particular expertise, which, incidentally, is necessary for a great variety of field workers.

3. THE DOCUMENT

This section is brief, but firmly unequivocal. It refers to the need for training and experience in the use of documentary material, both printed records and the preparation of questions of enquiry by letter or in person.

The document in European countries may involve the use of medieval sources. These occur in library archives, in some archaic form of the modern language, be it English, German, or French. The student of patterns of rural settlement or the beginnings and spread of towns in England, for example, will be involved in sources that are far more complicated than the original records of the Doomsday Survey, dating from the late eleventh century. The student of oriental affairs, must laboriously master the relevant language(s) before he can handle any records, past or present. Without so doing, he is unlikely to produce any significant contribution to knowledge. This is a task of long scholastic dedication.

The preparation of sets of questions relevant to a line of enquiry may well involve the mailing of thousands of *pro formas*. Such was the case with A. Demangeon's investigation of the regional characteristics and distribution of farmsteads in France noted above. Similarly, questions to be asked of a peasantry regarding their agricultural practices need to be carefully, simply and directly worded so as to get consistent and mappable replies. This is a skill which most of us learn by trial and error. Nevertheless, it can be cultivated in considerable measure by formal training and exercise.

This leads to a final comment. Whatever the corner of earth in which one operates, familiarity with the language of the people is essential. This does not mean merely the passing of a language test for a Ph. D. which is designed to be (though rarely is) an *entrée* to the professional literature. It means familiarity with the language so that one can meet the people with real understanding and without the frustrating intermediary of an interpreter. Further, one requires a knowledge of the culture and history of the group among whom one works, and also an appreciation (if not agreement) with their *mores*. The whole question of the use of documents and the techniques of enquiry, by circular or verbal interview, is a skilled technique that is essential to every social investigator who draws his materials from dead documents and living people.

4. THE MODEL

We have already reviewed the meaning and impact of the quantitative analysis of spatial phenomena (pp 32-36). Discussion will be limited here, to those aspects that are particularly relevant to the understanding of regionalization. For purposes of clarity and brevity, I follow again the book by Peter Haggett noted on p. 34.

The role of the model in the study of regionalization is very diverse. This approach leads to the study of spatial movements; spatial networks of routes; nodes or centers as clusters of population in terms of their functions; sizes; and spacing; and, hierarchies of nodal centers. It also embraces other hierarchical arrangements of spatial systems, such as political entities, or natural divisions of relief, soil, climate, or vegetation. These are the skeleton of the spatial system and the movements of persons, goods, and ideas that bind them together. There are "interstitial zones" around and between the skeleton which are conventionally studied from the viewpoint of land use. These form the mosaic of unit areas that are area continuities or "density surfaces." Their study that varies in its problems with scale, is concerned with the characterization of the substance of uniform surfaces (e.g., and agricultural system, a commercial or industrial system and its hierarchy of units), with the recognition of their limits (gradients of change) and what Haggett calls "the ratio level of measurement," that is, the measurement and fixation of limits and classification and determinants of "land use zones."

Regions take the form of homogeneity of one set of criteria (uniform single factor regions) or as composite complexes (uniform multiple factor regions). Such associations may be nodal around a focus, or organized as an entity (such as a political area). They are to be measured and located and explained in terms of process in time and space. Their locale and uniqueness can only be partially understood from mathematical formulae. Human entities are the expression of "social awareness." They expand and contract through the vagaries of place and time. The fact that they are "misty" (Haggett) does not dispose of their reality in human usage, past and present. Regional identity is naturally "misty" and no amount of quantification will convince a population of the regional sphere to which they belong or should adhere, or of which they form a part. Such a claim is mathematical determinism. A penumbra around a core area is as much a reality in the disposition of spatial groupings as is the "core area" itself, be it city or cultural hearth or politico-geographic nucleus.

Some method is necessary to resolve the wide zones of overlap in the fixation of regional boundaries. This has been partially resolved in recent years by the use of quantitative methods. A further problem lies in placing minor administrative divisions into a particular regional class in which they are grouped together by certain similarities regardless of location, or by consideration of contiguity of location. The latter goal may be reached by measuring the similarities of contiguous units, in which correlation coefficients for each unit area are measured to establish the degree of regional association with respect to a specified series of characteristics.

So much for theory and no further. It will be abundantly evident that equipment in model building techniques is a basic requirement in the study of spatial systems. However, the quantitative analysts need to be reminded that their brand of expertise simply has to be geared to the objectives of regional enquiry, namely, to the modes of segregation of spatially arranged phenomena over the earth, and, more specifically, to the modes of spatial association of human phenomena in their relations with the covariations of the physical and biotic habitat.

5. REMOTE SENSORY PERCEPTION

Special comment is needed on the role, present and future, of remote sensory perception on the knowledge and use of the earth's surface. The representation on maps of the surface of the earth has advanced far from the imagery presented some 50 years from aircraft circulating at low altitudes. Great strides were taken in mapping on large and accurate geodetic scales during World War II. Maps were produced by millions of aircraft "sorties" and also by radio communication with places beyond the reach of the senses of the recorder. Today, the whole earth has been photographed from earth satellites. The photographs, when reduced to a scale of some four miles to one inch, reveal, by color and shades, the most remarkably accurate reproduction of variations of relief, vegetation, land use, and patterns of human occupance.

It is certain that in the future other methods of earth imagery will develop beyond the use of the optical camera. Active attention is now being given to "remote sensing" of environment. Infrared rays are also being used for the recording of atmospheric conditions. Unlike the camera, the infrared sensor can penetrate the shadow of the dark half of the earth, although it cannot penetrate the clouds. Radar imagery permits overviews of sub-continental magnitude. It permits the tracing of terrain patterns over great distances; and overviews where timing is critical (to overcome darkness and weather). Moreover, the methods of terrain reproduction from properly equipped aircraft is far less expensive and more rapid than ground survey for the production of topographical maps. Underdeveloped areas could be rapidly surveyed by this method with mosaics of the whole country. From them can be derived the exact locale of specific phenomena, such as areas suited for irrigation, mineral resources, courses for new roads, or sites for industrial plants. Such surveys can also be used for the preparation of maps on small and medium scales.

This field is beyond the scope of undergraduate training, though there should be some exposure to its possibilities and findings. Certain graduate schools may choose to specialize in this field, as well as in computer use. It must always be remembered that these techniques are to be directed to the objectives of regional investigation.

Chapter 6

REGIONALIZATION OF SOCIAL PROCESSES

1. GENERAL

Regional groupings of places with similar or interrelated human attributes are dependent upon the operation of human forces. These reflect what Preston James has often called "the attitudes, objectives and technical abilities" of persons, not as individuals, but as members of social groups. I stand by this aphorism as a guideline in evaluating the regional concept. These are the ecological forces that condition the modes of life of human societies which in turn are manifested in the habitat which they inherit and transform. These regional associations fall into three categories: economic; cultural; and political. There is clearly much overlapping between them; but attention is focused in turn on each for the purpose of this brief discussion.[1]

[1] In the search for a summary of the social forces of regionalization as currently viewed, I frankly confess my indebtedness in writing (rather than by reference to my own published works) to short articles by three scholars. Their ideas closely correspond with mine, but they have expressed them so much more succinctly. I refer to Chauncy D. Harris, 'Economic Regionalization,' *Geographia Politica*, Vol. 4, 1964, pp. 59-86; Hans

I begin by repeating the main points of previous pages. Regional associations of human phenomena fall into two broad categories. Uniform associations are homogeneous and spatially contiguous and continous with respect to certain characteristics of similarity. Organizational regions are associations of places with different characteristics that are made coherent by their common relations to a focal point or by the deliberate organization of a territory as a field of operation.

I have already stated that the content of a regional association, as an ecological matrix, is in part a structured whole of interrelated spatial parts. Its concern is not with the geographical distribution of one particular element, but with the association of interrelated elements as spatial structures. Individual items may be examined in their distribution as indicators of a number of dependent, and therefore geographically coincident, phenomena. For example, newspaper circulation is not examined as an individual item of behavior, but as an indicator of a whole series of habits and attitudes which the reading of a newspaper reflects. The ecological matrix contains four interrelated groups of phenomena: land; people; technology; and, organization. Each of these, considered alone and in association with the others, varies regionally. Regional variance is the expression in turn of three processes, adaptation to site; symbiosis of different places with interdependent attributes; and the absorption or rejection of innovations. This line of approach we shall pursue in the next pages.

Bobek, "The Main Stages in Socioeconomic Evolution from a Geographic Point of View," translated and reproduced in Mikesell and Wagner, *Readings in Cultural Geography*, 1962, first published in a German periodical in 1959; and, Jean Gottmann, 'Geographie Politique' in *Géographie Générale*, ed. A. Journaux, P. Deffontaines and M. J. Brunhes-Delmarre, *Encyclopédie de la Pleiade*, 1966, pp. 1749-1765. Each of these scholars have many important substantive researches to their credit that illustrate the problems and procedures of their respective fields, but these articles were found especially useful in highlighting the main trends of thought in the regional concept in recent years. See also Eugen Wirth, "Zum Problem einer allgemeinen Kulturgeographie: Raummodelle-kulturgeographische Kräftelehre-raumrelevante Prozesse - Kategorian," *Die Erde: Zeitschrift der Gesellschaft für Erdkunde zu Berlin, 100 Jahrgang, 1969, Heft 2-4,* pp. 154-193. This important new article is a general survey, with mapped examples, and embraces the American contributions, with a long bibliography, in its critical review.

2. ECONOMIC REGIONALIZATION

Economic regionalization reflects certain spatial aspects of economic systems. Uniform regions are concerned with what-is-where (a static view), whereas organizational regions are concerned with what-connects-to-what (the functional view). A third consideration is that *all* forms of economic regionalization change through time with changes in technology and ideology, either through the growth and spread of an indigenous notion or practice or by the acceptance of such innovations from outside. In these cases one is concerned with direction and limits of spread and the modes of spatial absorption into the cultural matrix.

Uniform economic regionalization includes production, such as agriculture, manufacturing, and consumption (or potential), which is usually referred to as the level of living of a society. Organized regions embrace both market-oriented activities (such as retail or all production or productive wholesale activities)or productive-oriented activities (such as fresh milk for a nearby market). Studies of uniform regions have been mainly concerned with production, and organization regions with market areas served through central places. Agricultural products and raw materials do not normally pass through central places, but use road, rail, or waterway, whereas a high proportion of consumer manufactured goods move to their markets through the distribution facilities of central places. Traffic flows, independent of central places, thus call for special consideration.

Uniform associations may be based on a single factor or a variety of interrelated multiple factors. A single factor association has a single criterion, such as the production of wheat. A multiple factor association means the co-variance of a number of interrelated single factors. The measurement of such a regional association may be undertaken by visual comparisons of maps; by field observation (see p. 68); by air photographs; by official statistical data mainly from census sources, e.g., percentage of occupied persons in agriculture, industry, and by services for small statistical units. A system of multifactor units, arranged into a complete hierarchy of four orders, has been worked out for the United States by D. Bogue by using 83 variables of census data of population, occupation, and income, and 75 agricultural characteristics. In recent years, statistical analysis has been applied to the study of the association among economic (and social) characteristics and natural conditions that vary over the earth's surface to evaluate, confirm or independently establish, regional boundaries with reference to the criteria found to be significant in factor analysis.

Numerous studies have also been made of the resource base. These have particular reference to agriculture and the natural conditions, on which land use must be inexorably based, no matter how sophisticated the technologies of production. This has been done on the basis of a predominant crop or crop-livestock combination. Other studies have examined "type of farming" regions on the basis of the proportion of farm income contributed by a variety of farm products. The land use survey in Great Britain, initiated and directed by the late Sir Dudley Stamp, is an important contribution in modern affairs, both in Great Britain, and by its extension to other lands throughout the world (see p. 70).

The regionalization of manufacturing has been studied, for example, by mapping the percentage of the population engaged in manufacturing to the total labor force for the smallest published statistical units. Much has been done with the measurement of the localization of levels of living by using various criteria such as amount of official (and hidden) unemployment, and various indices of social and economic conditions. This has been the purpose of my work on Southern Italy. Such studies range from a small country scale through continental, to worldwide appraisals.

The functional relations of cities to their catchment areas has been tackled from innumerable points of view and by field observation, interview, and questionnaires. Data have long been available in the atlases of firms in the United States concerning market areas (data on a county basis). Maps of traffic flows on a large scale are available in many states of America. Other data used are: freight rates by rail; passenger and freight movements; newspaper circulation (e.g., from the Audit Bureau of Circulation on a county base); and telephone communications and air traffic. Commodity flows have received much attention in recent years. These studies aim at the recognition of spatial patterns of the phenomena. Nodal points are found to fall into a hierarchical arrangement, a field of enquiry that was set on a provocative footing by W. Chrisaller, a German scholar, nearly 40 years ago. A geography of market centers and retail distribution (by Brian J. L. Berry) was published in the United States in 1967 in which the opening sentence reads: "The thesis of this book is that the geography of retail and service business displays regularities over space and through time, that central-place theory constitutes a deductive base from which to understand these regularities, and that the convergence of theoretical postulates and empirical regularities provides substance to marketing geography and to certain aspects of city and regional planning." The reader is referred to the book for the development of this theme.

An important measure of regional interlinkage refers to the ways in which plants in the same cluster are dependent upon each other. Many studies of this kind have appeared in recent years (using various kinds of location quotients). They are of great importance in the current trend for the state (as in Britain) to interfere in the choice and shift of locations of industrial employment. Take away a large key plant in an urban complex and it may not only add to unemployment and family dislocation, but could also impede substantially the efficient operation of hundreds of small enterprises that are, in some ways, associated with it in the provision of particular parts or the ready transport of a product from one plant to another for further processing.

3. CULTURAL REGIONALIZATION

Cultural factors reveal regional distinctions between human populations as socioeconomic structures, and between them and the environment they inherit and transform. These factors embrace language, religion, economy, and social structure. The social heritage finds expression in accepted legal codes. On the people and their institutions depends the architectural deposit in the milieus they occupy, be it a mosque, a Gothic church, a hotel of the railroad era, a motel of the automobile era, a subdivision of fields, or a style of grouping of repetitive plans and architectural forms in farm, village, or town. By language I do not mean the distribution of linguistics. By culture I do not mean the distribution of different forms of bow and arrow. By social structure I do not mean individual social traits like matrilineal descent, newspaper circulation, or literacy. I do mean the locale of *spatial complexes* of these individual phenomena that are relevant in the life and organization and habitat of groups of people. Research into individual phenomena demands the skills of a linguist, cultural anthropologist, or a social ecologist, who is simply using a geographical method in localizing his data. There is, of course, absoutely no reason why an investigator should not pursue such a course if he so chooses. However, the regional approach focuses on the cultural matrix, rather than on the geographic distribution of its individual items, although this, without question, may be the means to an end, which is reached independently or by borrowing.

The distinctive cultural characteristics of human groups have to be identified and located as to place and distribution. Explanation of these characteristics, however, is not only a matter of understanding them as they exist today. They embody traditions, origin, spread, and regional coagulation. These have emerged from the past, more often than not in remote times, and by doubtful routes that are fascinating to speculate upon, but difficult to prove. Human societies have followed a path of development through time, and the phase of evolution has been stopped for some reason at times usually in the obscure past. Cultures and peoples have localized, with very distinct traits, in various areas of the earth.

The steps in the evolution of human communities as ecological complexes at the end of the 15th century have been examined by Hans Bobek of the University of Vienna. Since this time the indigenous cultures have had controls and contacts imposed upon them by the spread of occidential culture and technologies—400 years from Western Europe, and in the 20th century from the United States.

The following elements, writes Bobek with reference to the earlier period in 1500, enter in the matrix of human societies, past and present.

(1) Modes of livelihood
(2) The social hierarchy
(3) Demographic structure
(4) Settlement patterns and forms, and other manifestations of culture in the landscape.

These items occur in all human groups, in all places, and at all times, in interconnected spatial associations. Their development and spread, disappearance, or absorption, change through time. This entails the study of the origin, distribution, and spread of individual cultural elements, that are significant as pointers to the ecological complex, or to the association of several of them as a bundle of transmitted cultural traits. In a recent undergraduate text on cultural geography, Broek portrays the origin and spread of diffusions, by reference, for example, to domesticated plants and animals, metallurgy, and the plow. He also locates the "cultural hearths," that is the areas, in which associations of traits (by deduction and often from archeological evidence) are supposed to have had their area of characterization. Spencer in a similar text refers to the world spread of gardening, mining, and smelting. These writers follow the example set by Carl Sauer in his remarkable work on *Agricultural Origins and Dispersals, 1952.* Interest in these works center not only on places of origin (involving theoretical deduction with doubtful and often inadequate evidence), but also on the location and extent of the existing cultural patterns of human societies in 1500, as springboards for understanding cultural impact and possibilities of economic development today, against the complex of the inherited cultures. All these scholars, incidentally, are avowedly following the tradition set by Friedrich Ratzel before 1900, who, as they are well aware, but many others are not, was more a cultural diffusionist than a "naive environmentalist", as his English speaking scholars have assumed without personal reading of his works.

Bobek, in submitting the old notion of continuity of cultural development through history to the current findings of archeology and history, suggests the following sequence of cultural development among what we may call the pre-industrial societies as they existed around 1500. The spread of Man and his cultures has taken place throughout the world in much the same way as plants and animals. Primitive cultures have survived in remote corners. Evidences are found in existing cultures as well as in archeological finds that reveal the routes of movement. In certain areas there occurred a coagulation of traits to form a distinct culture complex which may itself have subsequently served as a center of diffusion, as, for example, Western European and Chinese cultures.

The phases of cultural development as listed by Bobek are as follows (modified):

1. Food gathering.
2. Specialized collectors, hunters, and fishermen.
3. Clan peasantry, based on sedentary settlement with smallgrain cultivation.
4. Pastoral nomadism that apparently emerged as a distinct mode of life from the sedentary cultivators economies and localized typi-

cally in grassland areas.

5. Autocratically organized societies (feudal included) of sedentary cultivators.

6. Early urbanism and rent-capitalism, the latter meaning dependence of a property owning class upon the rents acquired from their dependents.

7. Productive capitalism, industrial society and modern urbanism, which in the last two aspects carries us to the spatial organization of contemporary societies.

These kinds of cultural structure are mapped for the world as of 1500. It was a task of every freshman student who attended an introductory course in geography at the University of Leeds, to copy this map and pursue as far as time and interest would permit (in subsequent years) the complex nature and characteristics of each of these cultures. This served as a base for the measurement of modern changes and the classification and mapping of contemporary cultures as economies and as technological and social complexes.

From the various forms and extent of the world's cultural realms in 1500, I turn now to the world of today. Through 500 years, there has taken place an enormous extension of Man's occupance and control of the earth. The world has been changed by the colonization across seas by emigrant European peoples; by the control of occidental over non-occidental societies in Africa and Asia; by forceful shift of peoples from more accessible coastal lands (as in the development of plantation farming in southeastern Asia, sugar and cotton in the southern States, with imported labor from the other side of the Atlantic); by the increased efficiency and speed of transport across the seas; and by rail, and (in the 20th century) by road over the continents; by the voluntary migrations of peoples, either across the oceans to lands where they pioneered; or by continental shifts by choice or force; or by "acts of God" (mainly famine); or, as in western Europe and America, by the daily journey to work by rail or car, whereas over most of the world peoples stay put and move only by foot.

It has been a great temptation for writers in recent decades to give the impression that indigenous peoples have become embroiled throughout the world in the network of trade, the technological potentialities, the rising expectations, of the occidental so-called "Industrial" or "Democratic Society." This glib line is emphatically wrong. The impact of the Industrial Society in the realms of the indigenous cultures is varied in nature and strength and, indeed its innovations are often rejected.

There are populations over large areas of the Old World and Latin America (to say nothing of Anglo-America and Western Europe)where peasant agrarian societies with their subsistence economies and indigenous *mores* are still overwhelmingly ethnically centered; with self-subsistence cultivators making up to 80 percent of their workers. They are remote from the flows of goods of commerce and new ideas; far from a railroad; far from a motorable highway. Vast areas are still remote from the orbits of cities or the carriage of goods to and from ports, far from the reach of electricity, that on arrival (as is happening in sectors of India) phenomenally transforms thousands of isolated villages by the provision of light at night, loud speakers for news, and power for the workshop. There are vast areas in which people rarely see a paper or go to school, and, in which the amenities of civilized living, the market place, the doctor, the school, the place of worship, are far away. These facilities need to be pumped into central places in order to meet the daily needs of villagers in squalor, illiteracy, poverty, and sickness. Over extensive areas the *mores* and shibboleths of tribal societies prevail and are already in headlong conflict with the lack of any accepted *mores* where people swarm into the appalling squalor of gigantic urban agglomerations without shelter, water, light, or sewage. All these are cultural desiderata that are very relevant to the measurement of cultural regionalization. They vary regionally and need urgently to be measured and mapped throughout the earth wherever human groups live.

Worldwide cultural realms have been mapped, and used as a basis of general interpretation by many authors. Bobek's scheme for 1500 is the most effective springboard for such study. Many others have been made over the past 50 years (beginning with Alfred Hettner) in order to reveal the enormous changes brought about by "the Europeanization of the earth," as it has been called. Authors naturally have their personal assessments; but there is a remarkable uniformity in their choice of major realms. It is a relatively simple pattern, since it is so basic. The major realms are: Anglo-America; Western Europe; Latin America; Black Africa; the Moslem Lands (North Africa and Southwestern Asia); Sino-Japanese Realm; Southern Asia (the former British dependencies in essence); Australia; and Pacific. It is in the nature of things that there should be lands in which the people have been closely associated with two or more outside realms, involving infiltration of foreign cultures, economies, and political controls. Such are; the Moslem lands of North Africa; the Caribbean islands and coastlands; the Black-White domain of South Africa; and the diverse cultural realm of Southeastern Asia, both islands and adjacent mainlands.

Cultural regionalization goes much further than this. In any one of these realms there are subdivisions, be they in the "primitive pre-industrial" realms or the realms of "advanced;" technologies. Using exactly the same criteria as those formulated by Bobek, cultural regionalization reveals an intricate pattern of associations, based on social structure, economies, demography and density of population. Transform each of these statements concerning worldwide cultural criteria into the form of questions for application in a continent or country and one is presented with the realistic problem as to the character, causes, and consequences of cultural regionalization. What for instance in Africa is the impact on *mores,* or community cultivation in a village, brought about by the departure of young men from the closely knit communal village to the places of work in cities, where they may stay for months or even years? This is a formidable problem in the migration of natives from village to town in intertropical Africa. It is one of the concomitants of urbanization that makes a varying spatial impact with increasing distance from the centers of urban attraction. Or again, what is the range and the spatial impact of mass migrations of African natives brought about by the intolerance of the governments of new states?

I pursue this theme of cultural regionalization no further with reference to the "advanced" societies of Anglo-America and Western Europe, since here lies the nub of this book, and it will be taken up in the following chapters.

4. POLITICAL REGIONALIZATION

The regional concept examines the political area as a geographic or a spatial entity in relation to its coincidence or disparity with other areas of distribution that are relevant to the operation of its functions. The foundations of such study were clearly laid at the end of the nineteenth century (1897) in a compendious volume, *Politische Geo-*

graphie, by Friedrich Ratzel, the German geographer.

The political area, in this sense, in its intrinsic characteristics, may take two forms. The formal political organization may be the township or the parish, an intermediate province of some kind, or the state or the inter-state organization. In fact all states have a hierarchical arrangement of politico-administration districts. The people in an area may have political attitudes, based on a common heritage, and may aspire to some measure of self-government (that is, the establishment of a distinct political entity). This may involve annexation to an adjacent state or establishment of a new and independent state. There are numerous aspects to this whole question of cultural and political nationality. The regional concept is strictly concerned with the spatial aspects of political groupings, formally established, or informally in existence. The state or any of its subdivisions seeks to exercise (sometimes to enforce) its power and responsibilities on *all* the people in *all* sections of its political domain to the limits of its frontiers, operating from the nodal points of capital and subcapitals. Ratzel long ago pointed out that the state in trying to establish authority and cohesion faces its greatest problem in resolving the facts of regional diversity of land, resources, and people. The core and purpose of political regionalization is then the character and processes of the spatial organization of political areas in relation to the other geographic distributions that are relevant to political organization and cohesion. This concept has practical uses in the field of geopolitics and educational value as a mode of understanding national and international issues.

The regional study of a political area embraces the following aspects: Any one of the aspects may be of special relevance in particular cases. This does not in any sense prescribe a routine treatment but merely serves as an indicator of approach.

1. The political entity needs to be examined as a whole and with respect to its component parts, in regard to the task of organizing, protecting, and servicing all its population, wherever distributed, and all its territory, however remote from its centers of operation.
2. The political entity, large or small, has frontiers of authority (even if astronomically defined) and centers of operation. The center, be it capital or sub-capital (down to the county seat) has a role of government to perform as a headquarters in a prescribed area.

The choice of the capital, therefore, (as in the United States) goes through a "settling-down" process. This involves shifts of location through the competition of three contending forces: the need for access to the whole of the political area; access to the effectively settled, or populous, area (that may cover only a small section of the total area); and access to the world outside the realm of its political area. A capital may be central to the effective area at the time of its foundation, but peripheral to the political area, though located on a main rail route. Delhi and Peking occupied eccentric positions in relation to the territories of conqueror and conquered, though at the zone of contact of both. Washington at the time of its selection was centrally located to the coastal fringe of colonies; today it is eccentric in relation to the area of the union and the location of its main seats of population. Modern states have sought to locate their new capital focal to the effectively settled area, as at Canberra and Brazilia.

3. Frontiers are the geographical limits of the political area. They may be "accordant" or "discordant" with other geographic distributions, spatial movements, and attitudes. A frontier may precede the economic development and interconnections on either side of it, as on the Franco-Belgian border. It may be imposed, as after World War I in Upper Silesia, on an existing urban area in which people, activities, and services are intermingled. A vast urbanized area, or a port area, may lie astride the boundaries of several states, as in New York and other cases. Some boundaries in Europe have been fixed for centuries and still have accordances and discordances with ethnic distributions and natural features. It will often be found that a frontier runs along a mountain ridge, but in detail it does not do so and the summer pastures of villagers may lie on either side of the boundary. The iron curtain is not only a break between East and West Germany; it cuts across linguistic and family associations, and the flows of traffic to and from little towns near to it.

4. Within the political area, be in state or county, there may be marked regional diversity of land, people, resources, and attitudes that the state has to somehow synthesize. Poverty stricken areas, not merely poverty—but the places in which it is mainly concentrated—need to be localized and measured as a basis for action. Similarly, pockets of unemployment in relation to the general re-

gional employment patterns need to be measured and evaluated. Motivations, in character and strength, need to be localized, though it is difficult to do so. Such is the matter of the distribution of bilingualism in Wales or in Belgium. These differentiated traits are needed in order to assist the state to devolve its responsibilities, or provide a measure of self-government to part of its territory, or formulate proposals of "home-rule" and "federation."

5. The individual state, as a sovereign and independent unit or as a dependency, has relations with contiguous states and peoples. Such regional associations, that may cover a large stretch of the earth's surface, depend on ties of historical heritage, or similarities of ethnic, economic, social, and geostrategic interests. Such is the British Commonwealth, formerly bound together by the "seaway of empire" through the Mediterranean and the Suez Canal. Another example is the Arab League, an association of states in southwestern Asia and northern Africa, that have a common religion and social structure, a common location, commanding the routeways across the World Island (see p. 160), and contain some of the world's major oil fields.

6. The "iconography" of the state, as Jean Gottmann calls it, refers to the "state idea" as Richard Hartshorne expressed it. This means the social philosophy and policy of the state in its development as a political entity. This is the driving force and key to understanding the placement of frontiers and capitals (in the former case, for example, in the placement of frontiers by a victor over vanquished), and the modes of organizing and governing the state. Innumerable features of landscape and people in the Soviet Union are unique and distinctive and arise from the philosophy and purpose of its Communist government. The policy of the state gives the dynamic basis to all the preceding considerations.

Chapter 7

REGIONALIZATION OF NATURAL ENVIRONMENT

1. DEFINITION

The term "natural landscape" has been embedded in French *(paysage naturel)* and German *(Naturlandschaft)* for over 50 years. It is so defined in contrast to the "cultural landscape," which is the man-made environment or habitat, transformed through time from the natural landscape. The geographic concept of landscape has given rise to, and will always provoke, new problems and lines of enquiry. This is the test of the value and validity of a concept. It has, however, made little direct and sustained impact on Anglo-American scholarship. The English term is translated from the German, and, we believe, was first introduced in the United States by Carl Sauer in the mid-twenties. The pursuit of its goals temporarily (in the thirties) became the objective of a group of enthusiastic followers of Sauer who described themselves as "chorographers". I recall in 1931 the preoccupation of this group with the concept of landscape as developed by Sauer, and particularly by the German, S. Passarge. They endeavored to turn all spatial functional analysis of Man on the earth into the visible deposit in the landscape. After significant case studies on these lines (notably by James on the Blackstone Valley in Massachusetts (1929) and Broek on the Santa Clara Valley in California) (University of Ulrecht, 1932), the pursuit was abandoned as microscopic and intellectually unrewarding. The general trend since then, with a few conspicuous exceptions, has been towards functional analysis.

The concept of landscape is concerned with the composite of the land and Man's transformation of it. It deals with the interaction through time of both Nature and Man in their regional variations. Nearly 50 years ago, when I trained for an honors degree in geography in a British university, one approached the study of land and of Man's works on it as arbitrary abstractions of individual elements. These were examined as the result predominantly of *one* process. The landscape, as the physical earth and Man's transformation of it, received no attention whatever. This shortcoming lay behind the bitter printed disputes between W. M. Davis, the American geomorphologist (writing in this capacity), and A. Hettner and S. Passarge, two leading German geographers, before World War I. Davis interpreted the physical forms of the land as the chronological expression of *one* set of natural forces of erosion and deposition. He devised the famous formula in the interpretation of landforms of "structure, process, and stage." He considered that, in studying the configuration of the earth's surface, one should retreat to a dark room and produce an abstract concept of a process, and then go out into the field, and interpret the landforms in the light of the abstract concept. This is a negation of the regional concept. The German geographers insisted that the concern of the geographer is with the real visible regional variations of the landforms, as of other terrestrial forms, and that the characteristics of such unit areas are the product of various processes acting through space and time. The geographer deals with the real and measurable variations of the earth's surface. Albecht Penck, the great German geologist and geomorphologist, insisted on this in the mid-1890's in a classic work. Davis worked on the basis of a single hypothesis, which he sought to read into the landscape as he saw it.

The term "natural landscape" *(Naturlandschaft)* was originally used on the continent in antithesis to the cultural landscape *(Kuturlandschaft)* that is transformed by Man in the creation of his habitat. The impacts of Man on the natural landscape are evident, as Jean Bruhnes assessed them over 50 years ago in France, in the spatial deposit of human occupance. This deposit changes with the sequence of techniques and human groups—fields, farms, hamlets, towns, routes, telegraph poles, billboards, dams and water bodies, and all the other paraphernalia of human occupance of land. The natural landscape refers to the surface configuration and the surface cover of the earth that are the product of the natural forces of Nature, without any deliberate or accidental human interference. The cultural landscape refers to this landscape as transformed by Man. At some time in the past Man made his first impact on the natural landscape. In the Old World, this has to be projected back into the prehistoric past. A limitation can be placed on this backward look by the search for the landscape as it was before human groups settled permanently in it and began to transform it territorially from its natural condition. This has been called the primitive landscape in German *(Urlandschaft).* This question of delineation of the original landscape at the beginning of effective human occupance is relatively simple in North America, since over large areas the conditions can be traced in written records, and in many areas from human memory. In Europe it involves a search into place names, botanical evidence, historical records, and the placement of such data at the exact places of occurrence. This has a substantial and dedicated and very provocative research literature to its credit. The work of Otto Schlüter on the vegetation of central Europe at the dawn of occupance by the German tribes (500-800 A.D.) was published in the 1950's. Its researches covered 50 years and it is an outstanding contribution to knowledge of that part of the world.

There are, of course, many vague, indeterminate, and controversial transitional areas between the processes of Nature and of Man. The contrast between the desert and the towns is shifting. The impact of a smelting plant, emitting masses of injurious gases, affects and changes the wild vegetation in which it may be situated. Zones of vegetation reveal distinctive features with increasing radius from the plant. The usages of Man operate similarly in more civilized places. The country estate has its distinct ornamental landscape. The machines of technological Man and his complete disregard for Nature result in the destruction of wide areas of natural vegetation within the reach of his area of operation, although tribute should be paid to the highway engineer who makes scars across the land without visible impact on the vegetation through which the highway passes. Over vast areas where Nature rules supreme there are patches of human occupance—simple cultivation, or complicated stretches of mines and plants, be it in the Amazon forests of Venezuela or the deserts of the Trucial States. In other words, there is a spatial intermixture of natural landscapes and man-made intrusions, either as sprawling blots or linear strips. Nature also operates in strange ways. The surface cover of vegetation is not static, as the observer normally assumes; it is always subject to change in time. Undoubtedly one of the most destructive and changing natural forces is fire, that, once started, continues unabated until a natural condition or barrier checks it. It is often difficult to trace over vast areas just how the forces of Nature have operated to create a particular ecological formation of forest or grassland, or whether human occupance has also, in some way, been responsible for such changes. There is a total antithesis between the landscape of Nature and of Man, but there are many obscure grades that challenge the ingenuity of the scholar.

The human occupance of any land has to establish a working relationship with the terrain. Man also has to find some accomodation to the demands and opportunities of the sea. His attitude to the sea is largely conditioned by his techniques for sailing it and his desire to use its resources, or cross its expanses either by point-to-point navigation or by leaving sight of the shores for the unknown. Some three-quarters of the earth's surface is under water and only one-quarter is covered by land. Of these lands only between one-quarter and one-third are the continuous domain of Man, in which there occur fields, farms, routes, villages, and cities, stamped in a distinctive cultural image. This is the effective area of the lands occupied by the world's 3.7 billion people. The rest, three-quarters to two-thirds of the lands, remain as the domain of Nature's undisturbed forces—the ice field, the tundra, the coniferous and equatorial forests, and the deserts.

The seas are very relevant to the life and possibilities of Man in his use of the planet and the mastery of its distances. It offers fish for food, and a potential source of fresh water through desalination. It offers access to other shores, around which a people may group its domain (as in ancient Greece, or northern Norway, or medieval Venice), or across which it may find the means to traverse in order to reach other lands; and it offers currents and atmospheric conditions that may hinder or aid navigation. The littorals for these reasons, being most close to the occupied mainland, are of special concern to Man in matters of territorial occupance and control. Throughout the history of Man's organization of his habitat, the seas, according to their size, shape, and location, have served both as links and barriers. The recent published books of Carl Sauer on the Caribbean and the North Atlantic, *The Early Spanish Main* and *Northern Mists,* reveal the attraction of this theme. There is a geography of the seas, pursued as a distinctive end, apart from, although needing understanding of its physical qualities, that lie in the realm of the skilled oceanographer.

The lands of the earth as the permanent habitat of Man are our primary concern. Every piece of land occupied by Man, be it the most highly valued site in the middle of a city or a stretch of wild land in a desert or forest, has to be adapted somehow to the needs and modes of the occupants. The mode of use depends on the objectives and technical skills of the occupants or the society or state to which they belong. Just how land may be divided and organized for cultivation and what shall be grown on it, or how a specific site in an urban area should be used for building, and what particular conditions are presented by the site (bed rock of granite or land that is liable to flood, or liable to soil creep or faulting), all these requirements of site must be assessed, no matter how sophisticated the techniques of use. The demands of Nature set limits to the techniques of Man, be he the man of America, or the shifting cultivator of Borneo.

It therefore follows that all study of the physical elements of the lands of the earth, viewed in relation to the regional concept, have one of two interrelated objectives: first, the regional variants of the world's natural landscapes as the product of natural processes; and, second, the modes of use and adjustment of human occupance to the physical traits and location of the terrain. Regional study in any area, local or worldwide, has these consistent objectives. To reach these objectives understanding and skills in other disciplines is essential, be it geology, botany, anthropology, or economics. However, these specialized skills, exactly as in any other fields of enquiry, must be utilized and directed to the resolution and understanding of the questions raised by the regional concept.

2. THE SCOPE OF PHYSICAL GEOGRAPHY

Physical geography grew out of natural history. Indeed, during the nineteenth century, the two terms were synonomous. Kant regarded physical geography as the outer world perceptible by the senses—natural as opposed to moral philosophy—a world that included land, water, air, plants, animals, and man. This concept also dictated the content of Humboldt's *Comos,* in which there is a very cursory review of the races of mankind at the end of the work.

The rapid spread of the evolutionary idea in the sixties witnessed a change of interpretation. This new evolutionary approach in its relevance to the study of the physical features of the earth's surface was first presented by the great British biologist, T. H. Huxley, as a series of lectures for young people in London in 1869. These were published in 1878 as a book with the title *Physiography: An Introduction to the Study of Nature.*

The attitude and progress in this field were summed up among English speaking writers at the end of the century (20 years later) by the works of H. R. Mill in Britain and W. M. Davis in America.

H. R. Mill's *Realm of Nature: An Outline of Physiography,* published in 1892, is a study of earth processes, not of earth forms. Unlike Huxley's exposition, it *includes* plants, animals, and man, the life-forms being treated as derivatives from the physical (described as geographical) environment. Mill's view of "physiography" betrays the all-embracing mode of thought of supposedly interconnected chains of cause and effect. This is a faith that is just about as exaggerated as the teleological view of Ritter. Mill was evidently unaware of the distinctive questions of geography as set by Humboldt and Ritter. It is strange that the geography of Man should be appended to the closing pages of a classic work on the "realm of nature". This was the traditional approach in the late nineteenth century.

W. M. Davis limited the term "physical geography" (which he accepted in deference to the decision of the American Committee of Ten in the 1890's) in his *Physical Geography,* published in 1899, to the inorganic world. A smaller *Elementary Physical Geography,* published in 1902, however, follows the nineteenth century tradition by including living forms *in so far as they are derivative from the physical environment.* This approach is essentially identical with that of H. R. Mill. Davis' treatment includes the "geographical factors" in the struggle for existence, variations in the distribution of plants and animals, with "main causes" based on "changes in their geographical surroundings," the races of mankind as dependent on "the separation of the continents by the oceans, aided by certain mountains and desert barriers; peculiar species of islands based on isolation; climatic controls of distribution of plants and animals, and "savage tribes" and "the influence of geographical factors on history."

The term "physiography" was firmly established in the United States by the Committee of Ten as the study of the physical earth. In 1896 a volume on the physiography of the United States was published by the National Geographic Society, at the initial suggestion of Davis. This embraced air, water, and land. These were examined as the expression of processes on the earth's surface to form *units of land, rendered distinctive by the operation of similar processes on similar geological structures.* The term "physiography" was later adopted by a geographer, I. Bowman, and a geologist, N. Fenneman. One finds in their works a new approach that is truly geographic in research objectives and presentation. Bowman's *Forest Physiography,* published in 1911, includes landforms, soils and climates. Fenneman in his two volumes on the *Physiography of the United States* (1931), adopts the term, but considers it "a not very fortunate one," and although the study of the lifeforms is excluded from his basic conceptual framework, they are brought in "from time to time" as a "constant temptation." In these studies, then, the emphasis is on the explanatory description of land units as advocated by Davis. This is a distinct geographic objective in contradistinction to the studies of the previous three decades.

This concept of the physiographic unit is one of the main contributions of American geographers to modern knowledge. But the persistent attachment of "human derivatives" at the end of scholarly treatises on the physical surface of the earth has long been a deterrent in both America and Britain to the development of an independent geography of Man.

3. THE FIELDS OF PHYSICAL GEOGRAPHY

We now turn very briefly to the major advances in the twentieth century in each of the fields of study of the surface of the earth—geomorphology, oceanography, climatology, and biogeography—in their relevance to the regional concept.

The development of landforms through the work of running water on lands with different kinds of structure was worked out after 1870.

De la Noé and Emmanuel de Margerie wrote a book on the forms of the land *Formes des Terrains* in 1888. They treated landforms as the product of erosion by atmospheric agents on different "structural surfaces". The surface resulting from erosion of the latter is called the "topographic surface". The most important agent of erosion is considered to be running water, and the laws of river erosion are stated and the development of a river system is considered in areas of horizontal or slightly folded, intensely folded, and faulted strata.

This work was followed by others in the last decade. The chief of these were De Lapparent's *Leçons de geographic physique,* 1886, James Geikie's *Earth Sculpture,* 1894, and the works by Mill and Davis noted above. But the most important contributions, in which process is interpreted in relation to the form of the lands, were the pioneer works of two German geographers, Ferdinand von Richthofen and Albrecht Penck, both of whom began their careers as geologists.

Richthofen's work on *Führer für Forschungsreisende* (1884) contained the first classification of landforms. The book was intended as a guide to scientific explorers for the recognition and description of landforms in the field. The first part deals with field observation and equipment. The second, and main part, is a discussion of the processes involved in the shaping of the earth's surface, with the landforms classified according to the processes of formation, involving the agents of erosion and geological structure. The third part contains observations on soils, rocks, and the structure of mountains.

Albrecht Penck's *Morphologie der Erdoberfläche* was published in 1894. This is a great fundamental work. He distinguished the study of the morphology of the earth's surface from Geodosy and Geophysics, and uses, for the first time, the term Geomorphology.

Penck gives special emphasis to the description of the forms of the earth's surface, to morphometry (or morphography), as well as to the processes of formation *(Kräftelehre).* He also turned to the locale and grouping of similar forms into distinctive terrestrial groups. Indeed, his system of classification is *based on form not on process.* It would be absurd to claim that Penck underestimated, as a distinguished geologist, the role of process in the development of landforms. He insisted that in the geographical study of landforms, the primary emphasis should lie in the description, measurement, classification, and distribution of the forms of the land, from the smallest units of contiguous groupings, of different orders.

Active work in the study of landforms, that owed so much to the stimulus of Davis in the 1890's and 1900's, was followed by a second phase with the publication of the book by Walter Penck, son of Albrecht, on the development of slopes in 1924. This book made a negligible impact in Britain and the United States for it is difficult to read and understand, even to a German, and did not appear in English translation until 1953. A further advance since the war has taken place by the correlation of processes of development of landforms with climatic differences.

In considering the recent development of geomorphology, we must be ever mindful of the geographic aims and problems that were so clearly conceived by Albrecht Penck. It was also pointed out many decades ago by Mackinder in Britain that the field of geomorphology is peripheral to geography. Davis consistently made the same plea. Today, the geomorphologists, especially in Europe, are concerned with *process* rather than *form,* and in so doing depart widely from pursuit of the regional concept. We hear repeated cries on both sides of the Atlantic for a more "geographical geomorphology".

Oceanography emerged from the data collected by expeditions in the latter half of the nineteenth and the first half of the twentieth century. The findings of the former were brought together by the great German scholar, Gerhard Schott (1866-1961) in two works, one on the Atlantic Ocean (1912) and the second on the Indian and Pacific Oceans (1935). Preston James places Schott with Eduard Suess, the geologist, and Julius Hann, the meteorologist. Schott's "monumental work on the oceans completes the trilogy on land, air and water." He is credited by James with bringing "the geographic approach to oceanography." He attempted the first division of the oceans, based on a "synthesis of the most important characteristics and processes in the body of water and in the air above it." The criteria employed include configuration of the ocean floor, hydrology, climate, and the distribution of organisms. James' appraisal is flattering to the geographers, for there are few, if any, in this generation, who are familiar with the expertise of the study of the oceans, with the measurement of data at sea, or the treatment of data in the laboratory or at the mapping desk.

Climatology made little scientific progress until meteorological data throughout the world were taken, collated, and mapped. Humboldt devised the idea of an isotherm and drew speculative annual isotherms for the world in 1817. In 1852 K. Dove drew maps to show mean monthly temperatures and Supan devised lines of equal temperature range in 1880. A. Buchan in Britain published in 1869 his important treatise on *The Mean Pressure of the Atmosphere and the Prevailing Winds Over the Globe for the Month and for the Year.* The first very crude rainfall map of the world appeared in the German Berghaus Atlas in 1845 and the first isohyetal map of the world was prepared by Loomis of Yale in 1882 and was revised a few years later (1887) by Buchan. Herbertson prepared maps that appeared in the *Atlas of Meteorology* in 1899. Mention should also be made of the remarkable researches of British scholars in India, that resulted in Blanford's *Climate of India, Burma and Ceylon* (1889) and Sir Charles Eliot's *Meteorological Atlas of India* (1906). All these studies made possible the advance of scientific climatology.

Julius Hann (1839-1921) requires special note here as one of the great founders of both meteorology and climatology. He trained under the geologist Ed. Suess at Vienna and became director of the Meteorological Institute in Vienna in 1874, professor of Meteorology at Graz in 1897, and professor of Atmospheric Physics at the University of Vienna from 1900 until his retirement in 1910. Hann edited the *Meteorologische Zeitschrift* from 1866 until his death in 1920 and in it he brought together all available weather data for stations scattered over the globe. He also wrote two celebrated *Lehrbücher* and a standard handbook on climatology. Robert de Courcy Ward at Harvard (who took over the teaching of meteorology from Davis) translated these works for the English speaking world. As Brooks has said, "he put climatology into American geography."

The first attempt at climatic classification awaited the mapping of the relevant data. Down to the end of the nineteenth century the latitudinal insolation zones first defined by Aristotle were still in general use—torrid, temperate and frigid zones—although it was realized that winds, rainfall, temperature and pressure departed widely from this frame. In 1879 A. Supan pointed out that the torrid and temperate zones should be more realistically delimited by critical isotherms, rather than by lines of latitude. A few years later (1884) he divided the earth into 35 climatic provinces by subdivision of the hot belt (defined by the mean annual isotherm of 68°F), the north and south cold belts, bounded by the 50°F isotherm for the warmest month, while between lay the north and south temperate belts. (This was used by Herbertson as the major framework for his major natural regions of the world.) This rather crude division was quickly followed by the work of a second great founder, Wladimir Köppen (1846-1940), a German meteorologist of Russian birth. His first paper on thermal belts (1884) was based on the requirements of plant life. In 1900 he submitted a classification of climates, based on the association of temperature and moisture measured against the requirements of plant life (Köppen had studied under the great botanist, A. de Candolle). This was further developed in 1918 and expanded in a book on world climates in 1923. Köppen continued his distinguished work in the thirties, by editing with R. Geiger an international series entitled *Handbuch der Klimatologie.* After 40 years service with the *Deutsche Seewarte,* he retired in 1919. Subsequent research in climatology has in large measure been guided by Köppen's work.

Biogeography embraces, by general usage, the geography of plants and animals. It excludes (though logically it should include, as it did in Ratzel's usage) the geography of Man. The lack of data on a world scale, as in climatology, was the main deterrent to scientific advance. Desultory attempts were made to organize the distribution of plants and relate them to physical determinants. Fundamental, although factually lacking, was Humboldt's remarkable *Essai sur la géographie des plantes* in 1805. He regarded the vegetation cover as a whole, not in terms of individual plants, and recognized terrestrial zones each with "a natural physiognomy peculiar to itself." He thus clearly distinguished geobotany from plant geography.

In the second half of the nineteenth century efforts were made to relate plant distributions to environmental conditions in a physiological sense. A. Grisebach, however, clearly envisaged the nature of a plant formation in the physiognomic meaning, and this is evident in his book of 1875. A. de Candolle, beginning with the geobotanical viewpoint, turned later in 1872 to a view of types of vegetation over the earth as "physiognomic sectors of the landscape." A definitive work on plant geography was A.F.W. Schimper's *Pflanzengeographie,* published in 1898, and soon translated into English. The ecological approach, the study of the plant community in relation to its habitat, was first developed by E. Warming of Copenhagen in 1895 and quantitative methods of studying vegetation were expounded by

F. E. Clements of the United States in his *Research Methods in Ecology* in 1905. These works remained standard until the publication by the British ecologist A. F. Tansley in the twenties.

Schimper defined the essential aim of plant geography to be "an inquiry into the causes of differences existing among the various floras." He writes that the character of the vegetation on any part of the earth's surface is dependent on climatic factors. The main plant associations coincide with climatic controls, whereas, local variations are due to edaphic factors. A third factor of importance is the migration of plants in the past. This set clearly the goals of plant ecology.

Zoogeography presents the same kind of problems as plant geography. In the pre-evolutionary days, it was assumed that each area emerged as the result of separate creation and the task was primarily one of description and classification. It was about 1860 that Darwin and Wallace published their views on biological evolution, and then there rapidly emerged a dynamic approach to the study of zoogeography, guided by theories of evolution and dispersion. The growth of paleontology in particular encouraged study of the processes of development and dispersal whereby the present distribution of animals emerged. The regions of P. L. Sclater in a work published in 1858, were generally accepted, especially in Wallace's *Geographical Distribution of Animals* in 1876. However, surprisingly little progress was made. The study fell into disrepute and little serious attention is paid to it even today.

"Regional study" in zoology is condemned by J. L. Davies in 1961 in the *Geographical Review* since it "obscures rather than clarifies causal relationships" (a view with which we emphatically disagree). The definition of a region, he writes, on the basis of everything in it, is considered to be of little scientific value. This is an attitude that has long since been discarded in Western Europe but clings like a phantom in America. Regional research, however, has taken on a new lease of life in recent decades, says Davies, through the adoption of the ecological approach. Attention is being turned, particularly to the genetic point of view and more emphasis given to boundary zones between faunal "regions."

Historical zoogeography was also in ill-repute a generation ago, since it used particular faunal distributions to support general theories, such as, the theory of continental drift. Since World War I "a more responsible attitude" has been apparent, associated with progress in paleontology and taxonomy. The ecological approach, the third major branch of this study, is almost entirely a development of the twentieth century, but may be noted here before leaving the theme. The first major attempt to formulate this field appeared in a German work by R. Hesse, *Tiergeographie auf ökologische Grundlage*, Jena, 1924.

Thus, today the two main branches of zoogeography are historical and ecological. The latter studies the environmental factors involved in animal associations. The former studies the time factor, but there is no clear division between these two approaches. Moreover, each approach may refer to the habitat on a local scale or to a continent in a major "biome." This highly specialized field requires expertise in ecology, paleontology, and taxonomy, and a geographer would have to be competent in these areas. This observation is equally applicable to the study of other regional variables of landscape and society—of plant ecology, human ecology, geomorphology, and hydrology. The aim is ecological; the interpretation must be historical.

4. SOME CURRENT TRENDS

It will be helpful to note several current trends in the fields I have just outlined that have particular relevance to the regional variables of the face of the earth. We live in an era of specialization, and the techniques of the geomorphologist, the plant ecologist, and the climatologist, have languages all their own. Many geographers are also seeking, on the same lines, to make themselves scientifically acceptable as "kings of space." Such a trend is laudable and should be encouraged. But the geographers should always keep clear, as Ritter urged, their own objectives and purposes. There is widespread concern about their failure to do so on both sides of the Atlantic. I shall briefly note several trends over the past 30 years.

First, there is general recognition that the surface cover of vegetation and the forms of the surface configuration are not static, nor the result of the operation of one universal set of forces. The regional variables of the natural landscapes are the joint product of varied natural processes—movements of the earth's crust, climatic changes, migrations and segregations of plants, etc. Moreover, there is recognition of the fact that, both in the field and in the lab, one must devise methods for the measurement of these processes, just as Albrecht

Penck urged 70 years ago. This means the use of simulation models and highly complicated mathematical techniques.

Three kinds of regional questions may be highlighted. First. What is the role of fire in the transformation of natural vegetation? What are the common ecological characteristics of tropical grasslands and to what natural processes do they owe their origin, spread, and present distribution? (There is evidence, for example, that the gallery forest in the valleys of the high interior plateaus of central Brazil, which is the realm of savanna grassland, is the product through recent geological time of both climatic change and earth movement with the consequent rejuvenation of the southern tributaries of the Amazon.) How can vegetation be characterized in terms of physiognomic forms, and maps of distribution be so prepared?

An important change in interpretation of landscape study in this generation, has profound repercussions on the operation of the regional concept. It is now recognized that the work of weathering and the consequent modes of formation of landforms vary throughout the world, and indeed in the same territories, through time, with changing climatic conditions. This is evident in two ways that again can be highlighted. First, there is active interest in the wide occurrence of landforms in North America and Europe that were shaped beyond, the edges of the main ice sheets associated with the Pleistocene glaciation. The areas in which these landforms are located are described as periglacial. The second trend is the interaction of natural processes in the generation of landforms, climates, vegetation, and the recognition that the main overall determinants of the worldwide processes are climatic, as regarding both landforms and vegetation.

The results of this generation of researches are brilliantly assembled in a recent French publication called *Géographie Générale, Encyclopédie de la Pléiade,* edited by André Journaux, Pierre Deffontaines and Mariel J. Brunhes-Delamarre. I will not attempt to summarize its procedures, for certainly the first half dealing with physical geography should be translated into English. It begins with a presentation of the basic elements *(les Données).* These natural processes are dealt with under the headings of climatology, hydrology, erosion (introduction to climatic morphology), structure, and vulcanism. These processes are then examined in their interaction in the world's "natural regions" *(paysages naturels)* under the headings of the temperate lands (given more precise definition than the customary Aristotelian concept), glacial and periglacial lands, humid tropical lands, arid lands, and coastal lands. These essays were written by outstanding scholars in France. There is no such equivalent in the English literature. It reflects the long and strong tradition of enquiry that was established by De Martonne and Henri Baulig, and both these men were strongly influenced by personal contact with the American, W. M. Davis.

Second. A further trend is particularly notable of German work. This is the endeavor, which we have discussed in Chapter 4 (Section 3), to delimit and explain the association of natural processes in the formation of the smallest distinctive units in the physical mosaic of the earth's lands in their relevance to human use. Such a unit, in the ecological sense, has been referred to as an ecotope. There is substantial literature in this field, which was clearly established by A. Penck. It has been vigorously pursued by those who have followed him, notably Carl Troll, one of the most respected scholars in contemporary Germany. This approach is evident in French work, though not attacked with such systematic thoroughness as in Germany. Relatively little progress in this direction has been made in the United States, and yet, from a human ecological viewpoint, it is perhaps the most important challenge of the regional concept. In Britain, there has been a swing among younger geographers towards the ecological interpretation of human communities, but we still await a substantive contribution to the concept. On the other hand, geomorphologists in Britain are doing outstanding scientific work upon which it would be presumptious of this writer to comment. Their problems, however, have little if anything to do with the regional concept and to burden the undergraduate with their particular expertise, as is the case in many Universities in Europe, means an entirely different course of training that is demanded by the regional concept.

Third. There is a question to which the ecological approach can contribute as an urgent commitment. I refer to pollution. There is environmental pollution due to atmospheric impurities, noise (that can be measured by decibels), smell (that is especially engendered by the industrial cattle feed-lots in certain western states), contamination of water and soils. The regional investigation of pollution requires: first standards of measurement; second, selection of stations for measurement at specified times and under specified conditions; third, the mapping of the data, whereby one may then determine the areas of varied incidence of each type of pollution. Such research is laborious and involves elaborate organization of numberous records over long periods of time. Smog, stinks, and noise are social evils that are of differential regional occurrence in both city and country. This assessment is an urgent social responsibility of the physical geographer.

Chapter 8

REGIONALIZATION IN RURAL AREAS

1. DEFINITION

The regional concept in its relevance to Man's use of land is concerned with what are popularly described as the countryside or rural area and city or urbanized area. I shall consider regionalization in rural areas in this chapter, and turn to urban areas in the next chapter.

The regional variants of the countryside embrace land, land uses, and their associated rural settlements. Land refers to the terrain. Use refers to the way in which the land is used, not only for farming, but also for forestry, mining, fishing, and recreation. This includes the variations from place to place of composite agricultural systems. Settlement refers to the spatial arrangement and sociogeographic organization of farmsteads, hamlets, towns, and routes. The population includes not only the farming families *(Primary Rural)*, but those who contribute to their needs in village and country town *(Secondary Rural)*, but excludes those who depend on the exploitation of other natural resources, or who retire in the country, or live there, but work in a city elsewhere *(Adventitious Rural)*.

The recording and mapping of these data involve field data and farm returns in the published form of census materials for small statistical areas. The use of this source material for the production of finished maps is determined by the limitations of scale—local (topographic), country and continent (chorographic), or world (atlas) scales. Each category presents its own problems of classification and mapping and interpretation.

There are four groups of regional variables of the countryside. First, there is the agrarian system. This embraces the disposition of the cultivated land—fields and strips in relation to the location of the place of dwelling and work of the cultivator; and systems of rotation, technical equipment, and the role of domesticated animals. Second, there is the use of the land on each of the fields, strips, or tracts. Third, there is the mode of disposal of the products, the ratio of goods consumed by the peasant and his family, to goods sold for cash, for the provision of food, clothing, shelter, health, education, and taxes. In other words, this means the relative importance of subsistence and commercial modes of economy. Fourth, there is the potential productivity of land. This depends on the physical characteristics of the terrain and the climate, and is measured against the minimum standards of technical equipment and levels of living that are acceptable in the country under investigation. This last comment is particularly noted here as a warning to western investigators in poverty-stricken areas, for they must learn to avoid ethnocentric standards of measurement. One cannot expect the peasant in Greece or Bengal to attain the same standards of living as the citrus farmer in California.

These four components, and the individual spatial elements of which they are composed, are interdependent although attention may be focussed on one of them. Each demands sophisticated procedures of selecting and handling the data. Problems and procedures will differ in the countries of western Europe or the United States, as opposed to states in tropical latitudes, where not only physical and climatic conditions are so different, but where accurate maps and local statistical data are often not available.

2. AGRICULTURAL SYSTEMS

An agricultural system is an association of agricultural practices, or, as the term is used in English, "a type of farming." This is not simply a matter of the distribution of particular crops, livestock, or implements, as was assumed a generation ago. One now seeks to distinguish the characteristics and distribution of ecological associations of these items and practices. The term "Corn Belt" was coined on the assumption that the distribution of corn gave the keynote to a particular type of agrarian economy. In fact, a variety of types of farming occurs in the area of the Middle West in which this ecomony is supposedly localized. Thorough statistical examination of crop and livestock associations by counties is a much more realistic measure of the extent and regional variability of agricultural systems. This ecological approach has received much attention at all levels over the past 30 years, far beyond the old routine of mapping individual distributions and finding out their relation to some physical condition of the land.

A worldwide scheme was published by the late Derwent Whittlesey of Harvard (and Chicago) in 1936. It is a valid and useful indicator of such study and the forerunner of many schemes of this kind. Whittlesey considered crop and livestock associations, intensity of production, disposal of products (consumption or sale), the buildings used to house and operate the farming activities. Working on such lines, and limited in classification and detail of mapping by the world scale of operation, and, moreover, by the paucity of data in many areas, he recognized 13 agricultural systems as follows:

1. Nomadic hearding (subsistence).
2. Livestock ranching (commercial).
3. Shifting cultivation (tropical rain forest; subsistence).
4. Rudimentary sedentary tillage (essentially like 3, but with fixed settlement, with some commercial crops, such as oil palm and cacao).
5. Intensive subsistence tillage with rice dominant.
6. Intensive subsistence tillage without paddy rice (dry grains and tree crops).
7. Commercial plantation crop tillage.
8. Mediterranean agriculture.
9. Commercial grain farming.
10. Commercial livestock and crop farming.
11. Subsistence crop and stock farming, resembling 10, formerly widespread in European Russia, but greatly diminished over the last generation.

12. Commercial dairy farming.
13. Specialist horticulture.

The mapping of these world distributions was achieved by piecing together maps produced on a continental scale. These were based either on statistical data or by inference, and the areas enclosed by lines (isopleths) that were adjusted to regional variations rather than to the arbitrary limits of the available statistical divisions.

There is urgent need for the mapping of agricultural systems on a consistent basis and scale. In 1949 the International Geographical Union appointed a research commission to undertake such a survey of land uses throughout the world, with the aim of producing a series of maps from original surveys on a scale of 1:1,000,000 with a basic and consistent system of notation. The initial scheme was as follows:

Scheme of Classification for the World Land Use Survey

1. Settlements and associated non-agricultural land
2. Horticulture.
3. Tree and other perennial crops.
4. Cropland—(a) continued and totation cropping; and (b) land rotation.
5. Improved permanent pasture, manager or enclosed.
6. Unimproved Grazing land, (a) used; and (b) not used.
7. Woodlands—(a) dense; (b) open; (c) scrub; (d) swamp forest; (e) cut-over or burnt over forest; (f) forest with subsidiary cultivation.
8. Swamps and marshes (fresh and salt-water, non-forested).
9. Unproductive land.

The scheme presents great problems owing to the diversity of systems of agricultural occupance under a great variety of physical conditions. Substantial experiments and changes have been made in a diversity of land surveys.

The Land Utilization Survey of Britain, that served as a springboard for the work of the Union's commission, is a remarkable achievement that deserves special comment here. It was almost exclusively the work of geographers, from the late Sir Dudley Stamp, who initiated it, through his many professional colleagues, and teachers in high schools, down to their young students, both in high school and in the Universities. The survey was completed during World War II as a matter of high priority. Every piece of land was surveyed field by field on a standard map on a scale of six inches to one mile, and the results printed and published on a scale of one inch to one mile by the Ordnance Survey. Accompanying these maps (for individual sheets or groups of contiguous sheets), are 92 agricultural monographs, which were almost entirely the work of professional geographers. The notation used in this full survey is shown below. A symbol was indicated field by field or equivalent unenclosed areas. These sheets were drafted in a variety of colors for reproduction on the one-inch printed sheets. The exact extent of the areas was retained by simple photographic reduction (six-fold). A number of the composite sheets for the whole country have been produced as atlas maps on a scale of 10 miles to the inch. The original field survey is currently being repeated, with some modifications in the notation. Over a 100 sheets are already published on a scale of 1:25,000.

The Land Use Survey of Great Britain

F Forest and woodland, sub-divided into high forest, coppice, scrub, cutover land; coniferous, deciduous or mixed; each shown by a standard symbol.

M Meadowland and permanent grass.

A Arable or tilled land and fallow.

G Market gardens.

H Heathland, moorland, commons, rough hill pasture.

G Gardens, allotments, orchards, nurseries.

W Agriculturally unproductive (buildings, yards, mines, cemeteries, etc).

P Ponds, lakes, reservoirs, dykes and streams.

These maps and monographs are the precursors, indeed, have served as examples, for many others that have been undertaken for small areas throughout the world over the past 30 years. Some are based on aerial photographs, others in firsthand field surveys, and still others on official statistics issued for tiny administrative areas (such as the parish in Britain, or the commune in France or, particularly the gemeinde in Germany). Today, one is confronted with a new challenge and potential of maps derived from earth-satellites. These are at a scale of 4 miles to 1 inch, and show the configuration of the ground and its surface cover and agricultural uses with remarkable accuracy and clarity. These maps reveal whole areas at one glance and cut out the long labors of the ground survey.

3. THE UNIT AREA

Special reference should be made to the so-called "unit area" in field survey (See Chapter 4). The term "unit area", refers to the smallest homogeneous geographic unit that can be used for measuring and recording the data of land use. This area is conditioned by the scale of investigation. If it is a question of direct field observation, one will begin in the field with map and pencils in hand, or with agricultural data by communes or townships on the cartographer's desk, or with the aerial photograph from an airplane or an earth satellite.

Land must be evaluated in terms of its physical characteristics. These condition what Man can and cannot do with it, how it may be used to the best economic gain and social benefit. Physical characteristics, with reference to human uses, refer to the slope of the land, the surface soil, the depth and character of the bedrock, and, the nature of the drainage (depth of the water table, surface run-off, evaporation, or sinkage). These must be measured in relation to the local techniques, not merely in reference to the extreme possibilities of advanced technology. These physical characteristics are closely interdependent, and are associated in such a way as to permit the recognition of small unit areas of terrain which have a uniform set of conditions. Such a unit area was called a "site" by plant ecologists in Britain in the mid-thirties. The soil scientists also use the concept of the catena since it gives the key to the locally distinctive kind of soil. Zoologists are now exploring the same notion in their use of the term "territorial imperative." It is especially in Germany that the concept has been developed. Indeed, the term "living-space" in reference to the spatial requirements of human communities, was developed by Fredrich Ratzel at the end of the nineteenth century.

The concept of the unit area as a physical unit is also applicable to the use of land. Land uses and agricultural operation are adjusted (or maladjusted) to the physical traits of the terrain. The potential production of a physical unit area will be set by the technical equipment, resources, and living standards of the people who occupy it. The terrain will also suggest the kind of equipment and input that may be introduced by any outside technical aid. This means that every acre of land, or more exactly every uniform site area, can be classified and measured as to its potential uses under the conditions of a given society.

A land survey involves, therefore, not only the classification and mapping of terrains and their existing uses, but also the measurement of potential use, and, in consequence, capacity to carry population. No matter how far, and in what directions, the agricultural populations of a state may expand, be it the United States, Britain, France, or Ghana, private operations and public authorities must establish working relationships to the possibilities of the terrain. Use, I repeat, embraces input, size and compactness of holdings, capital investment and labor, measured against financial output. This equation of agricultural occupance has to be balanced against the trends of population growth and limitations of rising expectations. The process of what the French call "demographic erosion," which may mean emigration of the young, or the emigration of the parents, or sale of their land at death, may result in a decrease of total population. This demographic change may then result in a transformation of land uses, economy, and ownership. Such changes may arise from hardship, but may end in the long run in better working relationships to the land and a higher level of living for those who remain. Whatever the trends, they must be adjusted to the regional variants of the quality of the terrain.

The mapping of the detailed configuration of the terrain and calculation of its capacity to carry an agricultural population (that is, the settlements of cultivators, plus the settlements of those who support them with services) was stressed in the 1920's by Albrecht Penck, the distinguished professor of geography at the University of Berlin, as one of the main responsibilities for scholars in a concerted worldwide investigation. The task remains undone. The World Land Use Survey is a major step in the direction of solving it, but it is only a beginning.

4. AGRICULTURAL PRODUCTIVITY

The measurement of the regional variants (that is, the variations from place to place) of the agricultural capacity of land calls forth two specific comments, one on land potential, the second on living levels.

Land potential has been estimated in Britain in terms of the uses best suited (within the British framework) to a terrain. A classification was arrived at in 1943 derived from the available land use maps we have already noted. Land was grouped into three major categories: first, good quality and highly productive (not too high, level or undulating, favorable aspect, deep soil, good drainage); second, medium quality; and, third, poor quality (low productivity, with inadequacies of slope and soil). Every field in the country, as shown on the Land Use Maps, could be, and was, placed in one of these categories.

The land capability classification used by the Soil Conservation Service of the United States is another noteworthy contribution. This scheme is concerned mainly with the dangers of erosion. It recognizes eight classes of land, four which are suited to cultivation. These are grouped as follows: (1) very good land; (2) land demanding moderate precaution; (3) land with considerable limitations, that demand careful precaution, especially against erosion; and (4) land with very severe limitations in use, including the best land in some semi-arid areas, and land in humid areas suited to forestry. The remaining four types of land are not suited for cultivation, although terrains of these categories may well occur in individual farm holdings. This grouping of terrains is not mapped in the United States with nearly the same accuracy and completeness as in Britain. It is rather a basis for evaluation.

Similar grouping of terrains are urgently needed in areas occupied predominantly by peasant agrarian societies. Here, well over two-thirds of the population are registered as directly dependent on cultivation of the soil for their livelihood, not to mention the other quarter to a third who support them in the villages and towns. There is also such need in the economically advanced countries. Certain lands become "marginal" as productivity increases, and technology reduces the numbers of workers and decreases the viability of small holdings, that are inadequate to maintain a family on an acceptable living-standard without supplementary income from outside sources of employment. The urgency of this need is fully demonstrated by the high priority now given to land assessment in Great Britain. The best terrains, in such a country, should remain in production and be preserved from the depradations of urban land uses.

States in tropical latitudes present distinct and urgent problems, pertaining to climate, land, and people. A land potential map of British Honduras, for example, shows three categories of land, one adapted to forest, a second adapted to agriculture, and a third demanding drainage or desalination, that is, high expenditures of reclamation before being suitable for cultivation.

In all such surveys, field mapping and photographic interpretation play a significant part, since local variations of soil are the best overall, and most readily observed, indicators of the physical characteristics of the terrain.

5. AGRICULTURAL POVERTY

The degree and distribution of poverty in an agrarian society expresses the resources of the terrain; the demographic trends; the prevalent and inherited agricultural systems; and the level of living. These together form a syndrome, that varies regionally from one section of a country to another. Any authority, be it a state government, an outside governmental agency, or a group of neighboring landowners, must know the regional variants of this agricultural syndrome, in order to bring effective aid to their people. Blanket legislation is rarely applicable to all parts of a state. Attention must be given to the regional variants of the condition with which the legislation is designed to contend. This applies to all kinds of legislation in all states, whether it be the relief of poverty in the United States or Britain, or in an agrarian society.

It was with the intention of measuring poverty and unemployment that the writer turned in the early 1950's to a firsthand study of an underdeveloped area. Southern Italy was chosen as the laboratory of field investigation, since it has an exhaustive census of agricultural and population data for each commune. This work will be briefly noted, and the references given, in Chapter 10, Section 7 on Regional Development.

The problem of poverty and malnutrition, coupled with the population capacity of agricultural land received much attention from the late Sir Dudley Stamp.[1] He pleaded for attention to these problems as did Albrecht Penck 50 years earlier.

"In recent years no problem has forced itself more insistently on world attention than the rapidly increasing pressure of population on material resources. The days of large scale exploration in the old sense

[1]Dudley Stamp, "The Measurement of Land Resources", *Geographical Review*. Vol. XLVIII, No. 1, 1958. pp. 1-15.

are over; the area of the land surface available for occupation and use by Man can be measured with an accuracy that becomes greater year by year. Although rich resources of minerals are still to be discovered and exploited and new sources of energy may be developed, the fact remains that the land surface is finite. Although the limits of cultivation will be extended into regions *(sic)* at present unused for reasons of cold, aridity, poor soils, inaccessibility, and the like, and although intensity of production will continue to increase, there is a maximum measurable extent to the cultivible area. Nevertheless, the ability of the human species to multiply is not yet measurable and must depend ultimately on the carrying capacity of the earth."

Stamp sought a measure of population carrying capacity, and a measure also, therefore of poverty, in what he called a Standard Nutrition Unit. This he defined as 1,000,000 calories of food *produced* or 900,000 calories *consumed* each year. (Our measure in southern Italy was one of *value* of production at current prices; his measure is one of dietetic requirement in terms of *calories.*) This provides a measure of both value of agricultural production, based on calorific content of production, and the level of nutrition. This measure, he continues, can be used in several ways. (1) By measuring the actual production and consumption it is possible to show how far the food intake of a given community falls short of the standard. (2) By relating total food outputs the area of land being used to support a given population under different farming conditions can be compared independently of the crops grown. (3) A measure of farming efficiency can be obtained. (4) By relating actual to potential use the capability of land to support population, that is, its "carrying capacity," can be measured. (5) By relating output to the unit of land over an area, such as a small country, where climate and type of farming are fairly uniform, the productive capacity of different types of land, that is, the range of "land capability" classes, can be measured.

This objective and its procedures are exactly in line with the independent examination carried out by the present writer in southern Italy.

6. SETTLEMENT: ITS SOCIOGEOGRAPHIC STRUCTURE

The term "country" is hardly an exact description of the agricultural landscape, since, as societies become more urbanized, services of the town penetrate more diversely and more deeply into the countryside, dominating farmstead, hamlet, and village. This urban impact on the countryside assumed definite and limited patterns in the last decades of the nineteenth century in the exclusive dominance of the railroad, fed by the horse and cart, but has taken on a new and rapidly changing role since the advent of the automobile and the ubiquitous road net. Yet, while large areas are subjected to a varying, but deep urban impact, there are extensive areas of countryside in which, though town-country relations are changing, they are still essentially rural, with distinct service institutions. There is the indubitable urbanized area that is dominated by urban land uses. There is a contiguous periphery of urban impact, variously described as interurbia, exurbia, suburbia. There are the areas, dominantly agricultural, furthest removed from the big cities, but served by the smaller country town. There are also the wild unsettled spaces that are being increasingly patronized by, and draw the bulk of their income from, the seasonal recreationist. There are finally, the "wilderness areas" in which land and life must be protected from the depredations of the human invader. These various types of area need to be defined and mapped, and the spatial processes of social service that are operating within them investigated. Following are some of the practical results of specific investigations, pursued in the interest of scientific understanding and social service.

It is common knowledge in western Europe that a "village" is normally the center for the activities of a territorially defined community area, such as parish, commune, gemeinde or gemeente. This area has varying shapes and sizes, with a radius up to several miles and a population from under 100 (in England) upwards to 10,000 or more (in Italy). All the dwellings of the commune may be concentrated in the village center. All may be completely dispersed on their own compact holdings and the center virtually non-existent, the church and other institutions being sited individually in the open countryside. The settlement may alternatively have developed in such a way that in addition to isolated farmsteads, there are several clusters of farmsteads or small clusters of service centers, called, in various languages, hamlets. These settlements are differentially distributed and react in various ways to the technological impact of modern urbanization, since they have different spatial characteristics and needs. The village community, whatever its geographic arrangement, has been affected by the growth and concentration of services in selected villages or small towns. Rural cultures are being profoundly affected by the impact of urban ways of life. The distinction between urban and rural, town and country, is blurred and difficult realistically to define.

I shall briefly draw examples of the processes in operation from several countries where essentially the same conditions prevail.

In Germany, the small country cluster, together with all the other settlements that make up the network of centers and routes, serves an area of about two to three miles in radius. Each serves almost exclusively the needs of the inhabitants in its immediate catchment area. Many village centers have services over and above those of their neighbors. They may be called "urban villages." Some of them fall into a somewhat higher functional order in the service of the countryside. They are seven to eight miles apart with an average population of about 2,000. Above these again are country service centers, with strong administrative functions for specific areas *(Kreise).* These are spaced 13 to 15 miles apart and normally have about 5,000 inhabitants. There are some four orders of larger centers, with the indubitable status of a city. These are outside our present interest, since, they do not by any means primarily serve the countryside, except with the most exclusive services.

There is, however, another small nucleus of rural settlement that does not enjoy the same functional status even of the small town. Many of these are inactive because of inaccessibility or competition of neighbors. Many have lost the weekly market they enjoyed at the height of the middle ages. Many, however, are still seasonally active, especially in mountainous or other sparsely populated areas that have too scant a distribution of settlement to warrant the growth of even small towns at frequent distances, but where, nonetheless, the inhabitants demand goods, services, and outlets for their products. These "auxiliary centers," as they may be called, are found typically on the borders of the service areas of towns (of different orders of magnitude), and also, as just noted, in thinly peopled areas.

France has a similar urban network, but the centers are smaller in population since the population they serve is more markedly agricultural and rural than in Germany. There are three kinds of commune centers that primarily serve the local countryside. The first is the cluster of farmsteads, with immediate everyday services and facilities

—*mairie*, church, primary school, several local stores and a café. The second is a larger center, that is often described as a *bourg*. It is particularly common in the southeast of France and is characteristic of the Mediterranean countries in general. Its activities are essentially the same as those of the smaller village communes. Third, large communes with dispersed farmsteads are typical of Brittany and the Massif Central. Here the center is a small hamlet of eight to 12 farmsteads with several shops and one or two institutions, such as a school, post office, or mairie.

There is a somewhat higher, though still country, order of center, the *bourgade*. This is the equivalent of the English market town and German *amtort*. Many of these have lost their livestock markets. Many serve as the center of a canton. On the average, they have about 1,000 inhabitants and are about 10 to 12 miles apart.

A center of a higher order has several thousand inhabitants and always less than one-third of its employed persons engaged in agriculture, but the services reach one-quarter to one-third. The population can reach 10,000 when swollen by industry or tourism. It has a more diversified range of services than the centers of the lower order. Its distinctive elements are some kind of college, a newspaper, small hospital, and an agricultural credit bank. These centers are about 20 miles apart.

In the United States, townships and counties were created in the pioneer days and their patterns were regionally adjusted as settlement spread from the Atlantic coastlands through the Middle West to the semi-arid and arid lands beyond the Mississippi. Throughout vast areas the quarter-section of 160 acres, section of one square mile, the township of six miles square, and the county 36 miles square, were surveyed according to the cardinal points. Farmstead, township center, and county seat (and even the state capital) finally settled down at a location where the catchment area (be it a farmstead, quarter section, township or county) could most effectively be served, depending on access to the farmsteads of the effectively settled tributary area by road, and access to the outside world by rail.

The advent of the automobile and the ubiquitous surfaced highway, plus the increasing complexity and multiplication of the functions of government and social service, have made these districts inadequate to cope with modern needs. What readjustments of spatial relationships, and in consequence, in the functions and spacing of service centers in the countryside are taking place? There is need for the reorganization of local government areas in the countryside, although the existing authorities (as elsewhere) are resistant and will make do with the existing framework as long as they can. There is need for much investigation.

Attention was first drawn to this problem in a classic study of a county in Wisconsin by C. G. Galpin, published in 1915 *The Social Anatomy of an Agricultural Community.* This revealed already at that date *(before the effective universal impact of the automobile)* the emergence of a spatial community more extensive than the small country neighborhood that depended on local traffic by wagon and horseback. The neighborhood is the first face-to-face spatial grouping beyond the individual farmstead and was initailly conscious of its entity by ethnic origin, isolation or the use of some common local institutions (school, post office, church). An alternative term used by rural sociologists is "rural primary group." The newly emerging center noted by Galpin, was a small service center. Galpin called it "the rurban community." His study was based on farm-to-farm questionnaires.

The same county was surveyed again in the same way by Prof. J. H. Kolb in 1929-30 and then again in 1947-48. These and other related studies in other parts of the United States reveal two trends in the sociogeographic structure of the rural community. First, some 50 years ago, the trade area was apparently the most effective denominator of the emergent "urban community," but it seems that in recent years the high school is a more effective factor of spatial cohesion in common social ties and group interests. Second, "village-country and town-country communities are becoming more differentiated and interdependent rather than increasingly self-sufficient and self-contained."[2]

The local neighborhood continues to lose its identity, particularly with the loss of local institutions, such as school, church, and store, that are being located in towns easily accessible by car or bus. Hamlets have declined, if not disappeared, all over the country. They tend to survive, however, in areas that are remote from town centers, where they continue to serve immediate, daily, and local needs. They frequently survive on the periphery of the catchment area of a town, or

[2]J. H. Kolb, *Emergent Rural Communities*, Madison, 1959, p. 11.

in an isolated, but populated area, where a town is some distance away.

A comment may be interpolated here on a most important sociogeographic trend and problem among small towns. In crossing the Middle West by highway, one is impressed by the changing appearance of the small country town since the advent of the automobile and the virtual demise of the railroad. Some at wider intervals of about 20 miles are flourishing. The pride of a town a generation ago was a multi-storied brick built hotel, together with good restaurant. Today, the chain stores and local department stores are well represented in the center and are evidently fulfilling useful and profitable services. This is also evident in the growth of shopping clusters on the outskirts of the late nineteenth century arrangement of comfortable homes and a variety of well appointed churches.

There are, however, many frequently spaced (about 10 miles) and smaller places, that show clear signs of decline, even of dereliction. They are run down and often stores are unoccupied. They may simply be going down-hill, not being able to stand up to the competition of a neighboring more active town that is accessible by car in a matter of 15 to 20 minutes. Many of these country towns are either suffering from competition, or they are turning themselves inside out. What is to be done by the "planner" with their old cores? Here is a vitally important social problem that should receive far more attention since there is no doubt that the future of society lies in the country town rather than in the amorphous, impersonal and costly sprawl of megalopolis.

To conclude, the basis of the urban network in Western Europe and the United States is a mesh of centers spaced at intervals of about six miles in the days of slow transport by horse and cart from farm to town, in the middle ages in Western Europe, in the 19th century in the United States. In the days of through highway traffic places were located at staging points, be they inns on the nineteenth century highway; depots on a railroad; or, motels on a freeway. A process of selection on the road-dominated mesh was put into action by the railroad. Since 1920, the automobile and truck have become paramount in both areas. Especially in England, the daily bus service, unlike Wisconsin, riddles the countryside to the remotest villages, as a social responsibility of public authorities. Nearly a third of the railroad tracks of Britain have been closed down by the state in the sixties. The development of transport and marketing organization, and the growth of new social services, have occasioned the concentration of functions in fewer centers. This involves considerable extension of the areas which the latter serve, and the diminished viability of the small centers and villages. This maladjustment of present economic, social, and administrative services to the distribution of towns is in the main a legacy of the past. It is reflected in fundamental and general problems of rural organization in both Europe and North America.

Administrative areas in the countryside bear no relation to the existing areas of economic and social orientation. The present system of administrative areas needs rational reorganization in order to bring it into closer geographic alignment with the areas grouped around the urban centers.

7. THE REMEDIAL SOCIOGEOGRAPHIC UNIT

In "social surveys" of rural areas, prior to the formulation of any scheme of reorganization, the distribution and character of all existing social services first needs to be thoroughly investigated. This requires systematic survey, as far as this is possible from the data available, of the distribution of, and areas served by hospitals, schools, cinemas, libraries, retail firms, wholesalers, etc. To determine the nature of the necessary reorganization of these services, i.e., to determine whether certain services are redundant or inadequate, selected "threshold" criteria need to be adopted. This question has received considerable attention in rural areas in the United States in recent years. This has also received attention in Britain and on the Continent in the post-war years and is now accepted as basic to the diagnosis and planning of town and country.

The question arises as to what is the ideal size for the smallest administrative unit. The "market district" in Germany, as defined by W. Christaller, has a radius of about three miles. He writes:

> "We find throughout the Reich that the smallest market district is centered on a place of the lowest grade which is a commercial center and a seat of administrative and professional services."

The service areas specifically referred to, in addition to those of a commercial kind, are police, telephone and postal districts, professional organizations, and medical services. Its center is the smallest town with 1,000 inhabitants. The corresponding feature in England is the small town with between 1,000 and 2,000 inhabitants, or even the urban village with 750 to 1,000 inhabitants. It is the "rurban" center the United States and the *bourgade* in France. This nucleus, together with the half-dozen or more villages served by it, form a district with a total population of about 2,000 to 3,000 in England. It seems that this size might serve as a suitable unit area in a new administrative system.

The population of the small country neighborhood is of necessity very small—200 or 300 people at the outside or, say, 50-100 families. The size of the smallest administrative units, established in the Middle Ages as units of social life and group organization, varies widely in different countries and districts. The overwhelming majority in Britain have less than 300 inhabitants. This is also true in certain districts on the Continent, but over large areas communes and gemeinden regularly have several thousand inhabitants. These contrasts lie largely in the circumstances of historical development and in the prevalence of different kinds of rural economy. The nature and distribution of the focal points will thus vary considerably from one pattern of population distribution to another.

An important contribution to this problem is a symposium of the Agricultural Economics Research Institute, Oxford (1944) edited by Dr. C. S. Orwin. This is an intensive survey of a particular rural area containing 12 villages covering 24 square miles in Oxfordshire, England. Three parishes had just over 1,000 inhabitants each and the remaining 12 had 150 to 350 inhabitants. A main conclusion of this survey is that most villages are too small to function as active seats of rural activity.

> "The village of a few hundred people cannot survive as a healthy organism. It cannot maintain any of the social services; it must send its senior, and sometimes all its children, away for their schooling; it must share the services of a district nurse; it cannot bear the overhead costs of water supplies, sewerage, or electric light; it has few shopping facilities; it cannot support the rural recreational organizations, cricket and football clubs, Women's Institutes, Young Farmers' Clubs, Guides and Scouts, and so on,

solely because there are not enough men, women, and children of the various age-groups to run them; it cannot give a living or a life to a resident parson or Free Church minister."

The late Professor C. B. Fawcett (my teacher and colleague), on the basis of the requirements of an elementary school in England, suggested a population of 1,200 to 1,400 as the ideal "residential unit," but this again in other countries depends on the minimum and maximum number of pupils and staff of a school. Dr. Orwin, in applying Fawcett's proposal, points out that the three larger villages in the survey area in Oxfordshire "approximate to the lower of these figures, and they confirm in many ways that this population can support a vigourous community life." The same writer favors the controlled development of industry in rural areas. Dismissing the idea of new industrial towns built round the factories as being antisocial and artificial, the alternative would be (he writes) to repopulate all the little villages within a certain radius of the factory instead of establishing "housing-estates" in the towns near the factories. "Villages thus enlarged by the influx of industry should find themselves emancipated from most of the disabilities from which small rural communities . . . are suffering today." This has been a normal trend in many areas of the Continent and is today being actively encouraged. It has not gone far in Britain, but is being pursued as a policy for industrial dispersal.

In all countries of Western Europe and in North America the spatial structure of the rural community has been subjected to continuing change by the new space dimension introduced by the truck, the car, and the bus. The establishment of small industries in peasant villages and market towns, the dispersion of urban population, whereby villages become dormitories, and the growth of "new towns," are profoundly changing the countryside, the functions of its centers, and so the web of spatial relations between urban center and countryside.

Chapter 9

REGIONALIZATION IN URBAN AREAS

The urban area may be examined as a regional structure from two points of view, first, as a spatial grouping as a whole, with respect to residence, work, business, public utilities, open spaces, places of entertainment; and, second, as an assembly of spatially differentiated but closely interdependent sectors or functional segments. I shall consider in this chapter these two modes of approach.

1. URBAN CONCEPTS

It was the distinguished British geographer and public servant, Sir Halford Mackinder, who, half a century ago, coined the term "nodality" in reference to the location of a town. From this basic idea there has developed a body of theory and empirical research focused on the distribution and modes of segregation of what are now called centralized activities. The concept of centrality holds that the services needed by the population of an area tend to segregate in fixed places. These places exhibit recognizable regularities of grade and spacing, depending on the density of population, the nature of the occupational structure, the level of living and the culture of the people in the area they serve.

There are two essential principles of centrality. First, centers are graded according to function and size from the smallest hamlet upwards to the metropolis. This gradation is, in effect, a continuum, but well-defined types may be recognized that form an interdependent hierarchy. Secondly, the system of distribution of centers is conditioned by the radial movements of traffic. Places of the same functional order tend to develop at approximately equal distances apart in areas with a uniform distribution of population and production.

A further concept closely associated with that of centrality is the economic base. This concept holds that the *raison d'être* of a settlement rests upon certain activities that bring income into it. These activities are called basic. On the other hand, there are activities of a highly diverse kind that support the basic workers and their families and may be described as services. The ratio of the basic to the non-basic activities can be measured in any particular town, as has been done for a number of American cities. It is a complex procedure, since many activities, such as newspaper sales and university enrollment, to say nothing of many industries, serve local, regional, national, and international markets. Moreover, it is essential to distinguish geographically between what is local and what is external. It yet remains to find a composite determinant of this ratio for urban areas. The basic-non-basic concept has been developed by urbanologists in the United States, as well as on the Continent, and has been applied to urban planning and specific business problems.

The concepts of centrality and the basic-non-basic ratio are both inseparable from the catchment area of the urban center. Every service and institution must be strategically located in relation to its clientele in order to work effectively. Each has a geographic range of collection and delivery beyond which its performance becomes inefficicent. Every central place, be it hamlet, village, townlet, town, city, or metropolis, emerges through the assembly of services and institutions. It also develops, in varying degree, as a seat of centrifugal and centripetal forces, that bring it into close connection with its surrounding area. By analogy with a magnetic field, this tributary area may be called the urban field.

With this concept is associated that of the city region. The relations of a city with its catchment area have complicated patterns. Each of these must be examined on its own merits, be it the range of goods or services, the impact of the city on land values and land uses, the movement of food supplies, the range of commuting to the city, or the range over which its industrial plants are decentralized. All of these have discrete areas and separate determinants. On the other hand, many of these associations with the city cover the same area, and, other things being equal, become more intense with greater proximity to the center. This results in a well defined zonal arrangement around larger cities in which all places have common sets of relations with the central city. A theory of the impact of the city on systems of agriculture was formulated by Von Thünen in Germany in 1826. This has had profound effects on scholars recently, who are concerned with the economic determinants of the range of market areas. The idea of the "milkshed" is well established in the United States. The idea of the "labor catchment area" is also breaking through. Local work areas, in which people live within walking distance of their work, be it the farm laborer who lives in a village or the textile worker in a terrace house next to the mill, are breaking down as work is found at greater distances. The homes of new factory workers are transforming the country village in Western Europe. We need to examine the spatial structure of local work-areas and the new trends of spatial orientation that are arising from the advent of the bus and the car. Such studies have traditionally sought after the origin of a plant's workers or the range of residence of the customers of a store. We need more meaningful methods of measuring the associations of people by place of residence with respect to their work, schools, and shopping centers. Above all, ways must be found of classifying these data and effectively mapping them in order to define the patterns of spatial connections on the basis of small districts within urban areas.

The concept of an urbanized area as a geographic entity is another challenging problem. It is a question of measuring and locating areal associations. The limits of the urbanized area may be defined in terms of the dominance of urban land uses. However, through the development of road transport, homes, services, institutions and utilities extend into a wide rural-urban "fringe." One speaks of the suburbanization of the countryside. There is also an exclusive kind of residential segment described as "exurbia." The American city is both expanding and exploding. Regional shopping center, school, church, and other services, may be up to 10 or 15 miles from their clientele, though accessible within minutes by automobile. This kind of area has recently been described as "interurbia" and may reach over 50 miles around a central city. Moreover, the daily journey to work by car permits people to live far out in the country though their work takes them daily to the city. About one-third of the farmers of America have some kind of off-farm work most of which is in cities. This urban impact reaches to a far-flung urban field, in which seasonal and weekend residences and recreation are increasingly expanding and even invading the desert as in California and Arizona. There is today an interurbia, an exurbia, and a suburbia. The urban way of life socially, economically, and politically, makes deep in-roads into the countryside. These each demand recognition as to their exact areal extent as well as to their common and distinctive characteristics.

It is now over 50 years since Patrick Geddes coined the term "connurbation" to designate a cluster of closely spaced towns. Both Geddes and H. G. Wells envisaged the time when many of these urbanized areas would merge, like pans of fried eggs. They have become "gargantuan scrambles." These various kinds of urbanized areas need exact geographic definition on the basis of varied criteria for many practical and urgent purposes of planning and government. This is partly a statistical problem, and a big step forward has been made by a group in the University of California under Kingsley Davis in giving a standard definition to the world's urban areas on the basis of the standard metropolitan area of the U.S. Census. It is also, however, a cartographic problem, in the sense that the pattern of urban expansion needs to be located and explained in its various forms, especially the intermixture of "rural" and "urban" in a new symbiosis. Such a contribution is made by Jean Gottmann's magnificent work on *Megalopolis*, the urban belt of the American Atlantic Seaboard. The geographic range and intensity of urbanization is basically an ecological problem.

It is appropriate to conclude with the concept of interlinkage. This refers particularly to the spatial interconnections of industrial plants in the differing stages and processes of production, although the concept is applicable to all forms of economic activity. The problem is to find ways of mapping and measuring spatial interlinkage between sections of a country, between cities, or between the sites of manufacturing concerns within the city and its surroundings. This is still largely a virgin field. The input-output model of economists is the main tool in use for such analysis, although this has been mainly explored with reference to the character, classes and patterns of traffic flows.

2. THE NETWORK OF URBAN CENTERS

The distribution of urban centers in any given area is the result of several processes. These operate in differing ways and with varying effectiveness through time and with changing technologies, with changes in the needs of the population, and with the nature and organization of transport, local government, and social organization.

First, there are urban settlements developed in relation to the mining of natural resources, or where bulky commodities may be economically assembled and processed. These are basic productive industries.

Second, there is a pattern based upon the provision of central services on a marketing principle, with the hierarchical arrangement I have already postulated. This would result in an even pattern of centers that form a hierarchy and spaced accordingly with hexagonal shaped market areas.

Third, there are the patterns associated with the demands of transport. The collection and distribution of goods to and from an area are effected through a port, or through stations along railroads, or stopping places on highways, be they the staging posts of the horse and buggy days, the railroad station of the railroad era, or strategic points and ribbon sites afforded by the modern highways.

Fourth, all occupied areas require seats of government and organization. All countries have a hierarchical arrangement of administrative divisions with specified boundaries, each with definite focal points. Such areas and centers were usually established at some time in the past and show a lack of adjustment to the present distribution of population and lines of communication.

It may be stated as axiomatic that the capital of an area is normally established in relation to two foreseeable sets of forces; first, the center of the administered area; and second, the center of the populated area. Such considerations prompted the location of Washington, D. C. at the time of its foundation when it was central to the settled areas on the Atlantic seaboard. Today, owing to the expansion of the Union, it has an eccentric position. The same principles were considered in siting the new capitals of Brazil and Australia. The operation of these principles is evident in the location of the county seats throughout the United States, county towns in England, the heads of departments in France, and the centers of *Kreise* in Germany.

Any settled area has a network of settlements that reflects the operations of these four sets of forces. Boundaries were normally imposed arbitrarily. Centers were located with respect to these various spatial distributions, after some shifting and choice and competition of sites. Time has brought a wider distribution of the settled area, a great increase in the demands of the population, and a vastly increased mobility since the advent of the automobile. We are now witnessing a process of readjustment of center to service area as mobility increases and the economic and social needs of a highly specialized economy increase. The central school in the small town supplants the little red school house in the small village. Local government units need to be recast in order to bring them into closer harmony with existing associations. The increasing complexity of society and the increasing dependence of the consumer, be he in town or country, call for a multitude of new services that are overwhelmingly concentrated in urban centers.

3. URBAN HINTERLANDS

I turn now to study of the hinterlands of the smaller towns of England.[1] The bus, that serves almost every village in the country, was taken as a criterion for defining the undisputed service area of each town. Centers were graded according to the number and frequency of their bus services to surrounding towns. The average area was found to be 81 square miles and the ratio of the population of the town to that of the hinterland was 3 to 5, the same as was found by Christaller in south Germany. Other indexes were worked out, such as retail stores per hundred people. In this way measures are obtainable on the basis of which one can judge the surplus or inadequacy of the institutions in a town to service the population of the town plus its service area.

These local accessibility areas were shown to closely correspond with the retail service areas of the towns, with the range of commuting when it is well developed, and with community of interest, as reflected

[1] F. H. Green, "Urban Hinterlands in England and Wales: An Analysis of Bus Services", 1950, reproduced in G. A. Theodorson (ed.), *Studies in Human Ecology*, 1961.

in the membership of social organizations. This work, prepared as a research project in the Ministry of Town and Country Planning, is a most significant tool to the planner. It can be extended to higher order centers to meet the needs of business and marketing organizations. Similar conditions are to be found in the countryside of the United States. This of course is a well established field of study and action in the United States that largely lies in the hands of market analysts.

4. THE CITY REGION

From the study of town-country relations, I now turn to the case of the large city region. Much work has been done on this aspect of study in recent years on the Continent; but there are still few substantive studies in Britain or America of the structure of an area in terms of its relations with central cities. This involves a conceptual framework and techniques that are evidently far beyond the naive notions of many planners, who still seem to be looking for an all purpose "region" that shall define the limits of a city beyond its administrative limits. Such a region just does not exist. My study of Leeds and Bradford in 1925 was the first attempt to distinguish between an inner zone of intimate and direct associations with the city, and an outer zone reaching to the limits of the competitive areas of neighboring capitals of the same order. In this outer zone there are few direct connections between the individual consumer and the central city, for the bulk of associations are with local towns of the lower orders.

I cannot allow this subject to pass without making reference to one of the most significant recent works in this field. It is a study of Lyon in France, the capital of a widely extended silk manufacturing and agricultural area. The author, Jean Labasse, entitles his book of some 500 pages "Capital and the Region; a Geographical Study of the Commerce and the Circulation of Capital in the Region of Lyon." The author traces the growth of Lyon as a banking center since the inception of its two big concerns in the 1860's and shows how the spread of banking to surrounding towns and villages was adapted to the particular economic needs of the diversified agricultural and industrial sectors within a radius of some 100 miles. He evaluates the interconnections of towns and cities with each other and with Lyon on the basis of banking data, telephone calls, and the like. One is thus able to perceive not only the outward reach of the city, but, what is far more important, the role that the banks played in the economic needs of its varied sectors. Here is a sophisticated study on the historical development of a city region.[2]

This approach leads us to examine the intricate ways in which there develops a symbiosis in the activities and ways of life of the town and the countryside around it. A French writer draws attention to three trends of this kind. One is concerned with the investment of capital by city entrepreneurs in the ownership of land and agricultural development of the surrounding countryside. There are also cases in which the modern town has grown in such a way as to sever its traditional connections with the countryside, especially where a large foreign element is introduced into the urban population. There is, thirdly, the new symbiosis that is developing, as in the United States and parts of Western Europe, with the spread of the urban way of life into the countryside. These are trends that can only be evalutated qualitatively in terms of development and change. They are particularly amenable to historical interpretation.

5. REGIONAL URBANIZATION

The great cities, in both America and Western Europe, are expanding on their peripheries at a phenomenally rapid rate. This is especially true of the United States, where the urbanized areas are spreading to the boundaries of the Standard Metropolitan Areas and even beyond them. This process of regional urbanization is producing continuous clusters of large cities interconnected by sprawling and heterogeneous urban land uses.

I have marked out in the United States and Western Europe the areas in which all places lie within easy reach of a well-equipped city. Cities with over 100,000 people were each given a radius of 20 miles. All other towns outside those radii with 25,000 to 100,000 inhabitants were given a radius of 10 miles. All places within these circles are within reach of work and service of a well-equipped city. This is a conservative estimate of the extent of the urban and suburban areas and of the range to which urbanization may spread. It obviously ignores the potential impact of the 40,000 miles of super-highways

[2]Jean Labasse, *Les Capitaux et la Région: Etude géographique. Essai sur le commerce et la circulation des capitaux dans la région Lyonnaise,* Paris, 1955.

that are being built in the United States to interconnect these areas. The Atlantic Seaboard belt extends through upstate New York and central Pennsylvania to the middle western states as far as the Mississippi, including the whole of southern Michigan. Cities in the southeastern states form a group of separate centers, but this is clearly one of the major urbanized regions of the nation. The Los Angeles and San Francisco regions are rapidly spreading into central California and even into the desert at an alarming rate. Houston and New Orleans are extending their tentacles towards each other, and to all practical purposes may be regarded as one urbanized region. The Puget Sound cities have a substantial size and though physically separate they are functionally closely interrelated. This is the spatial framework of urban growth for the next several decades. These are the major urban regions that will loom ever larger in the domestic problems of the nation.

It is of interest to compare the range of the urbanized regions of Western Europe when mapped on exactly the same scale.[3] There is a predominance of urbanized regions throughout England and central Scotland. The great axis of central Europe includes the whole of northern France and the Low Countries and a massive belt stretching through central Germany and south through the Rhinelands into Switzerland. Particularly noteworthy is the case of France, where the urbanized regions of the north and east are contiguous to those of her Common Market neighbors. The rest of the country is served by a number of evenly spaced medium-sized cities, each a regional capital and each a distinct field of urban association. Extensive rural areas are far removed from direct and regular participation in city life.

6. JOURNEY TO WORK

The most important single factor in the spatial structure of the modern urban community is the separation of place of residence from place of work. To examine this question one must have access to a thorough census of workplaces. This is now available in the post-war censuses of a number of countries in Western Europe. The lack of such essential data in Britain and America is one of the nightmares of every student and planner. Aided by the European data I have

[3] The maps referred to are reproduced in the writer's *City and Region*, London, 1964.

examined, for the smallest statistical units, namely, the equivalent of a few square miles and a segment of an American township, the degree to which these communities are dependent on outside employment, that is, on a journey to work outside their own administrative areas. Western Germany may be taken as an example. In 1950 14.5% of all employed persons worked outside the 25,000 local communities *(gemeinden)* in which they lived. These I call out-commuters. These data have been mapped. The map shows extensive areas in which the proportion of out-commuters to total resident workers is over 25 percent, and near some big cities, over 40 and even over 50 percent. These are agricultural villages located in the open countryside. They form part of an extended urban association, though they are well removed from large cities.

The causes of the varying geographic intensity of commuting in Western Europe are many and complex. They can be properly evaluated only in terms of the historical development of the areas concerned and through correlations with other relevant geographic distributions. The degree of mobility of people is not consistently proportional to the density of population; nor is it simply a question of accessibility, though access (by train, bus, bicycle or moped) is essential to get to work in a small town or a big city. Workers often cling to their native villages and the tiny plots of land inherited from their fathers rather than move to the impersonal life and higher costs of the city. Today in Germany one can see tiny bits of land that are left fallow by their owners who have found employment in a factory, but they retain the land as an investment against future adversity. Such unused land in Germany has been called "social fallow" and important work has been done on its distribution and causes.

This widespread separation of workplace and home puts a serious burden on the facilities and finances of the city, since it provides services for daily immigrants who do not support them. On the other hand, rural communities, with most of their workers employed in the city, often with a declining population, have an inadequate tax base to provide the essential services. There is need for new and wider areas as a basis for taxation. I envisage a typology of local government units defined in terms of the ratio between their income and expenditure that could be subjected to geographic analysis.

7. LOCAL GOVERNMENT AREAS

The whole question of the reorganization of local government units into new and larger areas, that shall be more closely related to existing areas of association of the groupings and organization of people, is a field that has some notable contributions. I would instance the pioneer work of the late C. B. Fawcett on the *Provinces of England.* This was published in 1919 in order to suggest major regional divisions that might be used as a more rational basis than the counties for a new system of local government and decentralization of authority from London. The author sought to define major divisions of England and Wales that were in fact coherent entities. He considered throughout the distribution of population, and their activities, movements, and associations, with particular reference to the orbits of association of the major cities. This book was reprinted in 1961, and is even more cogent today at a time when royal commissions have reported on the very problem of reorganizing units of local government. This is also a problem in Germany and France. Geographers in these countries for the past 50 years have been much concerned with the regional groupings upon which new major political divisions should be based.

8. FUNCTIONAL ZONES: WORK

Distinct, though often ill-defined, functional zones, make up the geographic structure of the urban area. They are recognizable in the ground plan and in the location and segregation of related activities, residence, industrial and commercial structures, and individual institutions that provide social services. Thorough studies of this kind in French and German date back to the first decade of this century. An outstanding American work in 1954 was concerned with the "central business district" of the American city.[4] This study sought to define the extent of the central business district as a distinct functional zone. It involved the use of blocks and the location of peak land value intersections. The activities that were mapped and used as a basis of definition were the retailing of goods and services and the performances of various office functions *for private profit.* Other lines of investigation await attention, such as the definition of what has been

[4]R.E. Murphy and J.E. Vance, "Delimiting the C.B.D." *Economic Geography,* 1954, pp. 189-222. See further comment in *City and Region,* p. 220 *et infra.*

called the "hard core" of the CBD and more specific delimitation of the zones of "deterioration" and "discard" that lie around it. The geographic pattern of land values is admittedly of importance to understand cities. It is not enough, however, to devise methods of descriptive analysis of existing uses, for the urban area is the changing expression of economic and social forces through time. The center of a city, is, in fact, its most diversified zone, in terms of buildings and uses. As the heart of the city, it contains many of the oldest buildings that are often nestled between ultramodern and multistoried structures. Many uses are not centrally located so as to reach the whole city; they are services parasitic upon these and have, therefore, a highly localized clientele of city workers. Historical interpretation is badly needed.

Much work has been done on the distribution, growth and functions, of business facilities in urban areas outside the central business district. Indeed, it is now popular to speak of neighborhood and regional shopping centers.

The growth of regional shopping centers is having repercussions on the functions and structure of the core, that has already shed much of its retail function and is becoming more a center for specialty goods and office space. The question is already posed for the planner—What shall be the future functions of the city core? The regional concept, when logically pursued, prompts certain essential questions about the C.B.D. What is the extent, growth and modes of locational grouping in this district? How has it emerged as such over the period of its development? How far is the term "business" justified as a measure of central? In what sense is it (or was it) geographically central? In what degree do its activities serve the whole urban area, for such is the meaning of "centrality," and this must be measured for all the grouped activities? What trends are taking place or foreseeable as a result of changes in the structure of cities?

9. FUNCTIONAL ZONES: INDUSTRY

Brief comment is appropriate at this point on the location and grouping of industrial plants in the fabric of the existing urban complex, as a springboard for diagnosis and action. It is one task to map the exact sites of existing plants. It is quite another matter to find a meaningful basis of classification in terms of geographical position in a spatial complex. Many plants have obvious forms in which they operate, such as gas works, coal mine, blast furnace, oil refinery. They have associated features that are offensive to the senses and generate heavy traffic flows. Many others, however, are not located in a separate building structure, but are intermixed with others on different floors of the same building. Still others occupy a single building over an extensive ground area. Numerous old brickbuilt buildings of several stories in industrial towns in England may originally have been textile plants, for example, but today accommodate (after interior structural alterations and new equipment) a variety of industries. Industrial plants have been normally classified and mapped in studies of cities (many of them as a springboard for planning) according to the goods they make, the processes involved, the numbers of persons employed, or their "nuisance characteristics." This conventional classification of industial sites needs reorientation and refinement in respect to community needs. Plants, for example, need to be considered in respect to the number of people they employ (which is a measure of aggregate traffic needs for transport to and from work). The kinds of traffic the plant itself generates is a basic consideration. Does it have (or need) access to railroad or main highway? Does it have (or need) loading and unloading yards attached to it? Industrial plants also need to be thought of as formal structures with respect to their horizontal and vertical components (ground area and number of storys). These are suggestions that would lead to better understanding of the appropriateness of a site in an urban complex, in terms of economic efficiency and social desirability.

The concept of "zoning" was first adopted in the United States in an ordinance in New York in 1916. Over the last 50 years it has emerged as a general planning procedure, and is both standardized and stereotyped on the lines of its initial objectives. The concept aims at blocking out the whole of an urban area into consolidated types of uniform or restricted land use, and is designed primarily to preserve desirable residential sectors from the invasion of "socially undesirable" activities. In consequence, large sectors of a city are reserved exclusively for particular uses. Industry, commerce, and even certain kinds of high density housing, are kept out of the most expensive residential sectors. The result is that nearly everybody has to travel daily to and from their work in a vehicle, either an automobile or a bus. During the last few decades, with the phenomenal increase in vehicular traffic (for the transfer of both passengers and freight) this geographic separation of major sectors in a city has resulted in an enormous increase of traffic flows and congestion.

These comments prompt two recommendations. First, there is need to think of industrial plants not only as physical structures and in terms of their transportation facilities, but above all as regards the amenities of residential districts and the convenience of their occupants. Second, there is urgent need for the crude concept and practice of zoning to be superceded by new procedures of measurement, based on community values. Many cities have vast areas reserved for future industry that bear absolutely no resemblance to the trends or possibilities of growth, and no proportioned relation in area to the rest of the urban area. One of these criteria would aim at easy access between home and workplace, so as to greatly reduce the daily journeys to work and the congestion of traffic flows. This principle is already in full operation in the recent mushroom growth of "regional shopping centers," which are located and equipped in order to tap an immediately accessible clientele. This trend is not as apparent with respect to business and industry. The practice of establishing large "industrial estates," as large and exclusive areas, employing thousands of workers, with an average of close to one vehicle per employee, needs to be critically examined. In certain cities in Western Europe, traffic congestion is reaching catastrophic levels and demands immediate action of some kind. Many enterprises could best be shifted from the city altogether and integrated in a new or expanded town, as is being done, for example, in Britain. Many others can be located (newly established or shifted from an existing undesirable site) in the midst of residential areas, if concerned with "light" activities, such as office work, or many manipulative processes. Their buildings can be tastefully designed and landscaped in order to do credit to an area rather than disfigure it. Such a trend would greatly reduce city wide traffic flows. In progressive planning circles, this is recognized as one of the major problems arising from the heritage of "zoning" in the accepted conventional sense. The costly erection of freeways around and through urban areas that are already sprawling is no solution, since it caters to the alleged inevitability of increase in the numbers of private automobiles, whereas every indication points to the need of mass transit as a civic responsibility in the interests of the common welfare.

This condemnation of existing practices of urban planning is based on the essential and fundamental needs of Man as a social and sociable animal. The history of urbanism demonstrates that these spatial groupings of community amenities, facilities and organization on a neighborly basis, transcend all the remote possibilities of technological invention. Living must be based on service to the whole community not upon the needs and whims of the privileged. A search for ways and means of reaching these goals of social justice is the objective in building new towns. These goals should similarly be applied in the reconstruction and expansion of existing cities. The stereotypes of yesteryear have left their blots on the urban landscape that it will cost money and decades to rectify.

10. FUNCTIONAL ZONES: RESIDENCE

The residential zones of urban areas need investigation in respect to their morphology and the distribution and movements of people. This field embraces the ground plan and the physical build on the one hand, and the distribution and movements of the population on the other hand.

Towns occur in geographical (regional) groups that reflect common traits of origin and growth. We drew attention in *The West European City* not only to such regional variants, but also to the spatial differentials within one urban area in the lay-out of its streets, places and blocks. The disposition and density of buildings and the styles of architecture characterize each historical phase of growth of an urban area. The ground plan is the expression of the changing process of historical development.[5]

The town, as an individual, expresses changing social values in history, concepts of planning, and the sequence of occupance from preceding patterns of property holdings through the purchase and subdivision of land for new buildings. There is much that is persistent in the design of cities, much that is very relevant to modern city planning, though all too often this is ignored by private developers.

The exact location of people and their social associations constitute

[5]See the author's *West European City: A Geographical Interpretation,* London, 1951, (Second edition, 1961), 582 pages.

what Gaston Bardet, the French planner, has called the "social topography of the city." This investigation deserves to be specially noted.[6] Bardet maps the relevant data for every dwelling in selected towns in France on a scale of 1:2,000. Two maps show the "day topography" and the "night topography."

This detailed inventory, it is claimed, permits the recognition of three persistent modes of geographic grouping. The first is the patriarchal or elementary "degree." This is a grouping of neighbors equivalent to a small country hamlet with five to ten families. It is a "truly biological social constant." The second is the domestic "degree." This contains a number of adjacent streets and squares with a total of 50 to 150 households focussed on a local group of shops. This is described as "a geographic-economic constant, the first properly urban element, where exchange and intercourse first occur." The third is the parish or neighborhood "degree." This is an association of several contiguous domestic degrees and corresponds with what is described in French as a *quartier* or *faubourg* or *bourg*. The public monument is one of its characteristic features. It contributes to the layout, life, and aspect of the city. It is reminiscent in size and development to the ecclesiastical parish, hence the name. It embraces some 500 to 1,500 households or a population of 2,000 to 5,000. These three geographic groupings tend to correspond with "the familial society, the economic society, and the political society." These are the units that should be used in the construction and reconstruction of urban areas.

Assuming this to be the essential sociogeographic structure of an urban area, what is happening to the sociogeographic structure of the areas of "urban sprawl" on the outskirts of existing cities and in the "remote subdivisions" in desert and highland of Arizona?

11. ENVIRONMENTAL PLANNING

Physical planning of country and city has felt the repercussions of Geddes' "regional survey," as well as the methods of analysis of Frederic Leplay in France a generation earlier, whose philosophy and procedures were so clearly reflected in the work of Geddes. There is

[6]G. Bardet, "Social Topography: Anayltico—Synthetic understanding of the urban Texture," *Town Planning Review,* Vol. XXII, October, 1951. Reproduced in Theodorsen, *op.cit.*

a long tradition of such enquiry in Britain among students of urban societies, notably the magistral works of Charles Booth's sociological survey of "London Life and Labour" (1902) and Seebohm Rowntree's classic study of poverty in the city of York (1901). There are also repercussions in America, notably the original "regional survey" of the New York Region in the twenties, and its complete revision (with changed problems and approach) in the sixties.

A remarkable fact here is the transference of the ideas of Geddes to the United States in the twenties by Lewis Mumford and the ways in which social planning and Ebenezer Howard's concept of the new town as a social entity took shape in the twenties, albeit as a "green belt town" or as a dormitory of a city, not as an independent community removed from its orbit.

Increased emphasis has been given since the twenties in Britain, to the concept of community and especially to the ecological clustering of human communities that should serve as a basis of reconstruction and construction of new towns *ab initio.* This was essentially the core of Ebenezer Howard's concept of "Garden Cities of To-morrow" at the end of the nineteenth century,[7] and it is the essence of the neighborhood concept, that found early conceptual definition by Clarence Perry in the *Regional Plan of New York* in 1929. The last undoubtedly reflected Geddes' ideas as transmitted by Benton Mackay, Lewis Mumford, Catherine Wooster, and Clarence Stein in the twenties. This social concept, as Mumford recently reminds us, enables the urban community to be kept in "human scale." However, it has since sunken into the background of American thinking, although it is a primary driving force in the philosophy of rural and urban reconstruction in Britain. Urban renewal is not merely a matter of destroying dwellings that are unfit to live in. These must be replaced with alternative accomodations for the displaced families and their institutions. There are usually strong neighborhood ties in condemned areas based on the long associations of people, common institutions, a sense of togetherness. The call of compassion and understanding demands that these facilities should be provided and that the new housing should be grouped in areas that should not only be healthy but also sociable places to live in. The elimination and replacement of derelict property is dreadfully urgent. But it is positively inhuman not to preserve in

[7]Reprinted as a paperback by Faber and Faber, London in 1965, with preface by F. J. Osborn and introductory essay by Lewis Mumford.

some way the neighborhood associations of local families who may live in squalor, but frequently prefer to stay where they are rather than be uprooted from their familiar environs and neighbors.

Between the wars in Britain the spatial diagnosis preliminary to the formulation of proposals for city and regional planning, followed essentially the procedures of Geddes. They were based on a standard presentation of geology, relief, rainfall, distribution and activities of population, etc. Geddes was internationally famous (especially in India) for this approach. A serious defect, however, in his procedure, was that it did not focus attention on problems of physical growth or of socioeconomic organization that might serve as signposts for remedial action. Such demands, however, dominate the objectives of physical planning since the thirties. One of the greatest planners of the last generation in Britain, namely, Sir Patrick Abercrombie, for 20 years followed the Geddes' procedure of presentation I have just outlined. But there is a notable change at the culmination of his career in the post-war plans, for which he was responsible, for the county of London (1940) and Greater London (1944). In these works the ideas of neighborhood and community as sociogeographic concepts are taken as guides in the future planning for the reconstruction of inner London and expansion on its fringes. The approach is ecological and seeks to focus physical planning on sociogeographic community needs.

Since 1945 regional expertise has been actively applied in Britain to the process of land planning. The examples given in the previous sections of this chapter were selected in order to demonstrate this very point. Sir Dudley Stamp was knighted for his public service on "the use of the land of Britain." In Germany, the contribution of the regional approach appears particularly in the work of the *Institut für Raumordnung* and its periodical *Raumforschung und Raumordnung,* both between the wars and in the last 25 years. The concept of centrality *(Zentral Ort),* as discussed above, has become a widely accepted springboard among planning authorities and individual investigators in that country. In France, a recent government report published in the United States, on *France: Town and Country Environment Planning,* outlines the purpose and procedures of this matter and its application to regional development in that country. The opening sentence reads as follows:

"The French term for the idea of environment planning, *aménagement du terrtoire* literally means 'organization of the territory' and, by extension, integrated development of the nation as a geographic whole. This idea is relatively new, having first been used in France 17 years ago, but it embraces a reality as old as man's settlement of the land. In a way, human geography is the history of the organization of man and his environment."

The central ideas in the regional planning of France, that follow in the pages of this report, are a direct application of the concepts set forth in this book. Several French geographers have played leading roles in this work of diagnosis and regional action. I would mention in particular the names of Gottmann, Philippeneau, and Labasse. The last named has recently brought out a substantial volume on *'L'Organisation de l'Espace: Élements de Géographie Volontaire* (1966, 605 pages). One could argue that this recognition has been somewhat tardy and ineffective in the United States, although one recalls the influence exerted by Carl Sauer (land use), Charles Colby (land development), and Gilbert White (watershed development) among a number of other less conspicuous but important workers in key posts. Nevertheless one gets the continuing impression, as an outside observer, that the distinctive disciplinary work of the regional concept (and I am not talking about those who become outstanding administrators in their own rights and merits) gets very little direct recognition and that many other specialists are doing the kind of work for which the regionalist is (or should be) eminently qualified. The overwhelming majority of practical men just do not know what a geographic training has to offer and for that the geographers alone are responsible and the current wave of enthusiam for quantitative analysis does not much help matters. It is for these reasons that I am prompted to summarise several of the areas in which the expertise of the regionalist, as set forth in this book, can be used in the diagnosis and treatment of city and regional planning.

First, "physiographic determinism" is an expression that has been recently used by a regional planner (of Scottish origin) in a plan for the development of an area in the eastern states. This is a very old bottle, with some new wine in it, which the geographers will find distasteful. It is one of the basic tools in the geographer's bag of tricks, which, in the United States, he seems to be doing his utmost to discard. The regionalist accepts and develops this concept, for Man, wherever he may be, as Preston James puts it, must establish some kind of working relationship with every little bit of land he used or occupies. The use of land, argues this planner (and I clearly support this view) *must* be adapted to the inherent characteristics of the terrain—slope, bed-rock, drainage, water-table, etc. Terrains need to be identified in local detail in any urban area, for example, in order to recognize and act upon the "do's and don'ts" of how the land should be used. It is often assumed that technology can ignore these dictates. There is abundant evidence in both urban and rural areas all over the United States of the abuse and misuse of land. The local variants of terrain need to be evaluated and mapped in their relevance to human uses and their possible consequences through human abuse. A regionalist should be trained to undertake this evaluation.

Second, every piece of land is involved in some kind of spatial network of human relationships. This net has been called an "ecological matrix" and we have already noted its four components of land, people, technology, and organization. These are all measurable and mappable, both individually and in association as ratios, be it in an urban or a rural area, be it in some part of the United States or in an underdeveloped land. The regionalist should be trained in quantitative techniques and map interpretation in order to expertly undertake this kind of evaluation.

Third, the modes for single or multiple use of land and the optimum location of spaces—fields, farms, factories, playing spaces, institutions, and highways—need to be examined in terms of spatial interlinkage and impact and the relation of one set of spaces to another set. This is the main theme of William Whyte's new book on *The Last Landscape* and I hasten to accept his challenge. If one maps with precision the spatially differentiated phenomena relevant to an intended new use, for example an institution or highway, one will be able to assess the pros and cons of a location. Facts relevant to a proposed freeway, that vary areally are liability to flood, land suited (or not suited) for housing, the catchment areas of schools and shopping centers, compact ethnic associations (for segregation is a fundamental trait of human social behavior), land that should be left in woods or too steep for road use. All these sets of data may be mapped separately and examined in association by the superposition of a series of tracings. In this way (and this is preferable in the last decision to any amount of sophisticated quantifying) there emerge areas or belts in which the course of a new freeway may be more or less or definitly unsuited. A freeway is a physical barrier to easy cross-movement, and should not cut across the existing patterns of social relations. This approach to regional analysis was used by the late Prof. C. B. Fawcett of the University of London, nearly 30 years ago. He called it the "sieve method."

I recall another study carried out recently by a professional regional planner with the aid of a committee of varied specialists. The assignment was to divide a whole state into areas that would be suitable for state-wide "planning." Hundreds of areal data were collected and recorded on cards for each county in the state and then fed into the computer. The state was regularly divided into counties and was mechanically mapped. The whole project was completed within one session. Considerable attention had to be given to the recognition of interrelated data that belonged to one association or system, for the variability of monthly rainfall,for example, has nothing to do with the extent of the retail trade area of a small town. The atlas of distribution revealed three kinds of maps. First, there were single distributions of the individual and unassorted cards in the pack, such as the yield of wheat per acre or the total annual rainfall, or the range of a particular consumer product. Second, there were distributions of coincident and interrelated items—multiple associations such as a system of farming or a retail trade area. Third, there were multiple spatially-associated systems, plus single items, that showed a high degree of areal correlation with each other that may be causally interrelated or may not. Incidentally, many of these areal variations of county data were not discovered until the data were mapped in this way.

It was discovered that "core areas" contained a high degree of spatial coincidence with sharply defined limiting gradients. Most of the state, however, had no marked gradients or centers of orientation. Where, in a required subdivision of the whole state, should the boundaries be placed? This was the final critical question. Until one knows exactly for what purpose the boundaries are to be used in this initial appraisal, it is quite impossible to draw consistent and meaningful boundaries on a sound basis. One may guess what the directive wants and select ones own criteria; a decision in practice that may well prove to be quite unsatisfactory to the planners.

The same procedure has been used recently in Britain for sorting out optimum locations for a 100 or more new towns, that should absorb new housing, rather than continue to cluster around the margins of the existing conurbations. How may potential sites of new towns be located? In order to answer this question, one needs to map out existing catchment areas of towns, locate and specify nodal points of highways, locate areas in which the scattered rural population is remote from service centers and available as labor for new employment. In this way potential areas for the siting of new towns can be specified. If the countryside of the United States were spattered with medium-sized cities (a policy which is being increasingly discussed), just where should they be located in terms of economic efficiency and social desirability?

Fourth, there is need for elucidation of the spatial interrelation of human groups as distinct segregations and as social groupings with particular focal points, such as places of work, shopping centers, and schools. The lines of flow of the periodic and aperiodic rhythms are: on foot (by young children going to school); by car (as the broad average means of travel), and by public transport. (The last is needed, as a public responsibility for the poor, incapacitated, or simply for those who choose not to use the private car. This neglected proportion makes up probably between one-third and 50 percent of all families). These spatial associations of areas, routes, and nodes, vary within the city and around the thousands of tiny urban centers that pepper the countryside of every county in every state of the Union. Every community should be served with the civilized amenities of the state, be it a junior college (designed essentially to serve an accessible commuting catchment area), a super-market, a library, or a hospital or other general medical services. Just where are the areas in which the population is *inadequately* served, or even served in superfluity? The analysis of the distribution of people in relation to their requirements of efficient service of social facilities (e.g. minimum size of a school or library) has become a primary objective in the provision of social services, in Britain, for example. This is an expertise in which the regionalist should be well equipped. In Britain he has rendered signal services.

The burden of this section is that spatial diagnosis in environmental planning is obtaining wide recognition especially in Western Europe as an urgent and basic need. A widespread complaint among planners is the rarity of persons with this kind of training from the universities in both Western Europe and America. A great deal of this work is being done by men who are learning and applying these concepts, especially by the planner or the social scientist without any realization that geographers have used these concepts for many decades. They are to be praised for this recognition of the expertise by pragmatically developing the techniques to meet their ends. The geographers are to be blamed on both sides of the Atlantic, and especially in the United States. They have not clearly developed in their student training, right to the doctorate level, a clearly enunciated conceptual framework and a clearly envisaged program of training, that will serve not as a strait-jacket, but as a springboard whereby these ends may be served. I have evidence from all over the United States that the ends of the regionalist, as expounded in this book, are not being served. And this is the reason why I have set my pen to paper.

To conclude, the regional concept as expounded in this chapter is finding ever increasing application to practical problems in the use and organization of space, both urban and rural; the conservation of natural resources; the water supply of cities; land uses; city and country planning; marketing; business; and, the reorganization of areas of local government. Social scientists are becoming increasingly involved in spatial problems.

The investigator may be deeply perturbed by what is going on, but it is not his function to act as critic or protagonist of a trend or situation. His function is to examine the structure of urban areas in the light of the spatial interconnections of urban phenomena, whether these be concerned with housing, utilities, services, commercial facilities or cultural and social institutions.

The individual categories of spatial phenomena relevant to an urban problem, such as the precise variations in the character of the terrain—lithology, drainage and slope—relevant to building above and below ground, or the distribution of types of industry or residence or service or population, or the location of playing-spaces, have to be mapped with appropriate criteria. Such study involves field observation, statistical techniques, documentary evidence, and cartographic analysis. The last is something more than drawing maps. It needs continuous experimentation in the laboratory for the discovery of meaningful distributions and correlations between them, and the permutations and combinations of varied areal criteria. In addition to the study of the character and causes of such urban associations we turn to the consequences. This needs yardsticks, either in the form of personal judgments or acceptable social values or clearly defined directives from the government official or the business man. From such studies one must be prepared to draw conclusions and make remedial recommendations in regard to the particular areal problems in hand, whether it be in defining new units of metropolitan government, or in siting new shopping centers, or in suggesting a new rationale of urban land uses. Appraisal of the character, causes, and consequences of particular groups of phenomena, in this case in terms of the areal arrangement of urban phenomena, is the essence of scientific method. Such is the regional approach to urbanism. Herein lies its justification, not only as a descriptive art, but also, as indicated by recent trends, as a fundamental research discipline.

PART III

PRACTICE

Chapter 10

REGIONALISM IN ACTION

A distinction must be made between regionalism as a "fact" and regionalism as an "act". The first, the substance of the last chapters, refers to the spatial associations of peoples and places that occur within and across the frontiers of states. The second refers to the consciousness of togetherness of human groups in particular areas and their desire and agitation for the fuller expression and recognition of their common experience and attitudes. We are concerned here with the second aspect, regionalism as a popular movement for the expression of regional consciousness.

In the political sense, regionalism may find expression in the struggle for self-determination. While the idea of the nation state has often been denounced as an anachronism in the modern world, the regional independence of sections of states has been increasingly recognized, in the post-war world, especially in Africa. Anguilla, with little more than two thousand adults, is the latest example, in its demand for independence from Nevis and St. Kitts, a tiny group of islands to which Britain has conceded independence. Small states, in order to be viable, must of necessity, depend upon other states for purposes of economic, technical, and strategic aid. The world is at present in a phase of increasing regional agitation for participation, and increasing interdependence of states with common ideas, ideals and geostrategic needs and economic policies. At the same time, in the older countries there is increasing need for more participation in government at the legislative, not merely the administrative, level, and hence for new forms of federalism and the delineation of new regions for effective representative government. I shall comfine comments to the three countries I know best; France, Germany and Britain.

1. FRANCE

Regionalism, as a popular movement for the fuller recognition in government of regional differences and aspirations within a state, had its beginnings in France. It emerged as a revolt against the centralization of power in Paris. France is often likened to an overgrown brain serving as the center of a body—the state—whose limbs are atrophied, very largely as a result of the deliberate plans of the revolutionary government after 1789. At that time, the historical provinces, with centuries of tradition and consciousness behind them, were eliminated, as were their organs of government in their traditional capitals. Their place was taken by a new hierarchy of administrative divisions, departments, arrondissements, and cantons, whose officials were appointed from Paris, rather than elected by the people. Regional traditions, folklore, and language, and the possibility of direct participation in regional government, were ignored, by the establishment of a system of government that remains to this day centralized in the capital.

The leaders of the regional movement sought to create new major divisions in place of the departments. In 1900 the *Fédération Régionaliste Francaise* was founded for this purpose with its organ in *L'Action Régionaliste.* It is not surprising that the movement had its beginnings in Brittany and Provence, the most peripheral and distinctive sections of France, in language, folklore, and traditions. Many schemes of regions and plans for the machinery of government appeared in the 1900's. World War I stimulated interest in the question and proposals were presented and discussed; but they were abortive. However, it has been necessary to regionalize a great many of the nation wide organizations, for which the departments are too small to serve as effective units. Most notable are the regional groupings of

Chambers of Commerce which were established in 1919 and, with some modifications, still are in active being. By 1939 administrative devolution was established for justice, education, military organization, and chambers of commerce. However, major regions as seats of democratic government, decentralized from Paris, have not been realized. Under the Vichy government during World War II regions were established for the emergency under Pétain. The country was divided into 21 regions (groups of departments) in the middle fifties, in accordance with the program of the National Plan for the regional habilitation of the state. General de Gaulle submitted the proposition of new major regions of self-government, and it is not surprising that his first public announcement to this effect should be made in Brittany. The major regions he proposed would follow the same pattern as the planning regions. This was submitted to a referendum on April 27, 1969. As the world knows, De Gaulle resigned since he did not get a majority of "yes" on this issue.

2. GERMANY

The problem of regionalism in Germany is based on a twofold need in the Reich: first, a radical overhaul of the inherited boundaries of the *Länder,* that often interlock and overlap in such a way as to bear no rational relationship to the orientation and interests and organization of human groups; and, second, the fact that in the past the state of Prussia dominated the area and population of the federation by about two-thirds, and its provinces needed to be reorganized so as to effect a balance between them and the individual *Länder*. The movement for such reforms assumed great importance in the Weimar Republic and exhaustive researches were undertaken by governmental bodies and individuals. Some advances were made under the Nazis (e.g., the extension of Hamburg). Further changes were made by the Allied armies of occupation (e.g. the establishment of Lower Saxony, Hesse, and Rhineland—Westphalia). The new federal constitution of West Germany in 1955 sought to continue and put into full effect a new geographic definition of the *Länder*. The relevant article in the Basic Law of 1955 reads as follows:

> "The area of the *Bund*, in consideration of its folk associations, historical and cultural ties, economic efficiency, and social cohe-

sion, is to be reorganized under federal law. The reorganization shall create States, which in size and capacity should be able effectively to carry out the functions allotted to them."

Further governmental recommendations and individual researches have been made to this effect. Regional referenda have been held in doubtful territories. Nevertheless, no action has been taken to cope with this delicate problem, that has enlisted the prodigious researches and efforts of public and private bodies for some 50 years. However, for numerous purposes the pre-war Reich was divided into major divisions, which were often much the same as, but not geographically identical, with the historical boundaries of the *Länder*. The problem of regional orientation of people, activities, traffic flows, city orbits, and the like, have long been matters of exhaustive analysis, and their materials would fill a library. Yet action on these decisions in democratic societies is very slow to be realized.[1]

3. BRITAIN

Regionalization of both government and planning is needed urgently in Britain. This is due to the excessive urbanization of the country, and the widespread impact of urban uses and urban ways, such as recreation, public utilities, demands for water, and pollution. There is also a longfelt need for recognition of the great disparities of economic structure and occupational balance, that call for regional treatment. Finally, there is need for revision of the local government areas that should be cohesive geographic entities, in order to be effective units of local government, and for more direct participation of the people in legislative and executive matters without the encumbrances and delays involved in the red tape of Whitehall. Yet, so strong is conservatism in local government, that there has never been anything like a popular regional movement to these ends. There are, however, growing and healthy trends in this direction. There are the increasing

[1]Special attention is drawn to Peter Schöller, *Neugliederung: Prinzipien und Probleme der politisch-geographischen Neuordnung Deutschlands und das Beispiel des Mittelrheingebietes* (Neugliederung: Principles and Problems of the politico-geographic spatial reorganization of Germany and the example of the Middle Rhine Area), *Forschungen zur deutschen Landeskunde*, Band 150, 1965. This is not named in the hope that readers will study it, but in order to indicate the thoroughness with which this whole problem is still being tackled, especially by geographers, in Germany itself.

demands for "home rule" in Scotland and Wales, a goal which Northern Ireland, for very special reasons, has rapidly and gratuitously acquired. We may also refer, in particular, to the case for "home rule" for the major "provinces" of England.

The case for regional revolution has never been a popular movement, but has long been a matter of concern to scholars and administrators. There are also many signs of regionalism in the national life, one of which is evident in the recent formation of new radio stations in the chief cities to cater to local and regional interests.

Action began in 1905 when the Fabian Society, the intellectual nucleas of the Labour Party, put forward the notion of a new set of regions for purposes of governmental devolution in a series of pamphlets called *The New Heptarchy.* They sought to define major regions in which the large cities would serve as centers for transportation, electricity and water supply. Scholars gave further attention to the matter between the wars, notably the geographer C. B. Fawcett, in a book entitled *The Provinces of England,* published in the *Making of the Future Series* (edited by Patrick Geddes) in 1919. World War II witnessed the formation of Civil Defense Regions (ten in England) designed to coordinate the administrative functions of various centrol departments. It has become increasingly apparent since the war that some new system of regional assessment, action, and government, with direct participation, is an urgent need for both economic and social reasons.

The country has long been divided into a multiplicity of major divisions for regional devolution. The great urban agglomerations, that are ever expanding (not growing!), need to be grouped together with their rural peripheries for the organization of transportation, education, water supply, electricity, sewage disposal, hospital services, taxation, and elective government. There are nearly 150 planning authorities today taking the place of 1,441 in 1947. Advisory reports on regional economic growth and land planning have appeared in plenty. But "regional planning," in the sense of groups of contiguous authorities planning and acting as a single unit, has virtually made no headway at all.

The Labor government has established regions for the assessment of needs and possibilities of economic and social rehabilitation and progress. It is becoming popular to speak of "London and the regions" as the theatrical world a generation and more ago spoke of

"London and the provinces." There is still a long way to go, for the administrative machine in London clings hard to its strings. However, the ends of these strings hold more than puppets. There is an urgent need, recognized now for over 50 years, for the establishment of a new hierarchy of local government divisions not only for greater economic efficiency, but also to meet the demands of more direct participation in local and regional government in the true meaning of democracy, rather than in the remote red tape rule of a central bureaucracy.

The British government stands on the threshhold of big and belated decisions. Two royal commissions have long been investigating the reorganization of the regional structure of government. The Maud Commission's report on local government in England was published in June of 1969. It proposes a reduction of education and planning authorities by one-half and authorities with house-building powers from over 1,210 to 61. The same commission also puts forward a case for eight elected provincial councils in England, and a considerable increase of powers of self-government in Wales and Scotland. The areas of the new authorities would be so designed geographically as to combine the towns and their surrounding country and they would be responsible for managing the services of education, housing, water supply, and sewage disposal. They would replace the county boroughs and county councils.[2]

The question of provincial government is the charge of a second commission under the chairmanship of Lord Crowther. Both matters, in one form or another, have been subjects of exhaustive public enquiry for the best part of 25 years. The problems they face have been the concern of a small circle of people since the beginning of this century.

4. INTERNATIONAL RELATIONS

The winds of freedom and self-determination are blowing throughout the world, not only within the states we have so far mentioned. Over

[2]Three large metropolitan areas, Birmingham, Liverpool and Manchester, would be divided into an authority for the whole area (planning, transport) and several district authorities (7,4 and 9 respectively) with responsibilities for education, health, and housing. While 8,000 parish councils will remain in an advisory role, the "rural" area and "urban" councils will disappear and be replaced by larger areas with about 250,000 people, with a radius of about 20 miles from a central city.

40 new states have emerged in Africa over the past 20 years. The sub-continent of India is now an assembly of separate states in one federation, while Pakistan stands alone in two widely separated geographic sections, one in the Indus valley, the other in the eastern section of the lower Ganges plain. The politico-geographic mosaic of southeastern Asia has not yet been entirely apportioned in accordance with the conflicting demands of its newly independent states.

These new states give expression to strong feelings of what we call today "togetherness" and to the desire, which is strong in the less developed countries as well as in the advanced countries, for more direct participation in government. The 2,000 adults, males and females, in Anguilla seek rights of self-government, independent of Nevis and St. Kitts, a union that was initiated by the parent government of the United Kingdom. The Ibos, ensconced in their "heartland," fought for independence of a regional federation of Nigeria in which they feared discrimination and oppression. Native groups in Africa have achieved political independence without bloodshed, except what has arisen since freedom from their colonial liberators. Others, like the Somali Republic, still search for group sovereignty for all their people, who are domiciled in the contiguous states of Ethiopia and Kenya. The south Vietnamese seek to preserve their identity vis-a-vis the north Vietnamese and maintain their claims persistently and vigorously under the umbrella of American military support. The French Canadians agitate in Canada, not only for equality, but for a much greater measure of independence, either as a province within a newly constituted Canadian federation, or, as advocated by their extremists, as a separate state, with sovereign independence. The examples could be extended.

All the peoples in these various areas must find accomodation with three internal demands, that are the very essence of their aspired freedoms.

First, they must find within their own frontiers, and from their own people, the personnel capable of leadership in education and government. It is difficult to imagine such an achievement among a total adult population of 2,000, but such is the problem that must somehow be resolved in Anguilla.

Second, these states must associate with others in order to achieve the ends which they cannot take care of themselves. They will naturally associate, for purposes of cultural, technical, economic, and s rategic purposes, with those states with which they have their closest interests, either by their own free choice or from external persuasion. The Anguillans, for example, turn first to the successors of the British in the Caribbean fraternity of states. Various groupings of contiguous states are already emerging in Africa, mainly to regulate and encourage their economic interrelations. There are many interstate, or, as they are commonly called, regional, groupings to which small states may turn. The British Commonwealth recently held a meeting of 28 government heads of states in London, a powerful force of concord and peace, if not of military strength. There is the geographical groupings of NATO, an association of states between western Europe and North America (United States and Canada). There is SEATO in southeast Asia, the Arab League in the Middle East and north Africa, and the Organization of American States in the western hemisphere. There is the grouping, economic and strategic, of the Soviet Union and its associates in central Europe.

There was the inter-war sphere of Nazi Germany in central Europe, and the "coprosperity sphere" of Japan in eastern Asia. Although both were considered to be undesirable trends by the "western" powers and led to World War II, there is not the slightest doubt that the dynamism of these two states must inevitably lead in the next decades to a repetition, it is hoped in more desirable form, of the extension of their "living space." Desirability is presumably to be measured in terms of freedom of choice and voluntary cooperation, without curbs from outside on the expression and running of internal domestic affairs.

Third, there is the fact that many small states occupy strategic geographical positions that are of special interest to other states, large or small. Many territories are disputed by two or more states. Such are the demands of Malaysia, Indonesia and the Philippines on northern Borneo, or the claims of India and Pakistan to Kashmir. Currently, we hear particularly of the rival claims of the Soviet Union and China to Outer Mongolia, the forceful occupation of the independent country of Tibet by China, and the intrigues of the Soviet Union in the Chinese province of Sinkiang. Superpowers, actively, though deviously, seek territorial expansion of their influence, ideological, economic, and strategic, among peoples outside their own frontiers. Such is the purpose of Soviet interests in the peripheral lands of its domain in eastern and southern Asia and in western Europe. Recently, China has renewed its interests on its traditional borderlands. Both the Soviet Union and China are spreading their nets to the new states of Africa. The containment of this territorial expansion has been a guiding principle of United States policy since the end of World War II.

Regional diversity within their frontiers is one of the major problems that confronts the governments of the new states in seeking to establish political control and popular concord to the limits of their frontiers. This diversity is very largely due to the arbitrary definition of political frontiers by the preceding colonial powers. One of the chief elements of diversity lies in the contrasted ethnic groups that are segregated in separate sections of the new states. Post-independence policies have tended to deepen these regional differences and contribute to the instability of the state. These ethnic traits include language, tribal association, religion and social structure. They are jealously maintained and guarded and in some respects are incompatible.

The migrations of peoples, voluntary and forced, from one new state to another, for fear of discrimination and death, has been appalling. The distribution of peoples in Africa has been changed by flight across the political frontiers. The same happened in the migration of millions of people across the new boundary of India and Pakistan. More than ten million were uprooted in central Europe during and after World War II and flocked into Western Germany.

There is another regional aspect to this situation in Africa. The native societies are being affected deeply by rapid change. The old traditions of the native cultures embrace 90 percent and more of the people who follow the practices of their forefathers and their economy is one of miserable subsistence. A maximum of some ten percent belong to an elite, and only about two percent of the total population have regular money income. The native Africans live in the widespread rural areas, whereas the wage earners live in the urban areas. The latter are growing rapidly, with the spread of commercialized economies. Folk (mainly males) leave their tribal villages and flock to the urban areas, where they live in squalor and are cut off from their traditional tribal ties, without being indoctrinated into any alternative codes of behavior.

Policies of land planning, urban growth, and social justice present problems of government that must contend with these deep seated and rapidly growing regional diversities.

There are also problems arising from the regional diversity of economies. Most of these states depend for their livelihood on the export of one or two primary products, and on the import of manufactured goods. The producers of a highly localized crop may desire policies favorable to them as exporters, but unfavorable to the people in other areas of the same state. Association of a localized commerical group with its neighbors across a political frontier may not be desirable to the population living in other sections of the state.

Appreciation of these aspects of the life of nations and states is essential to understanding of the politicogeographic structure of the world and the problems of government in its component states and their subdivisions, and in their international relations.

5. A GEOSTRATEGIC VIEW

One of the most influential books of this century is Halford J. Mackinder's *Democratic Ideals and Reality.* This book was first published in 1919 as a guide to the builders of the new world after World War I. Its significance was recently reaffirmed by the disaffection in Czechoslovakia, that was quelled by Soviet military occupation. This crisis reflected the struggle between the democratic *ideals* of a small state and the *reality* of Power Politics *(Realpolitik),* in a country that is located strategically in precisely the geographic zone between East and West that was so brilliantly interpreted by Mackinder.

Between the Wars, but particularly during the period since 1945, Mackinder's tenets and warnings had an enormous impact on political scientists and statesmen in their views and action on world strategy. The book did not receive much attention after the Treaty of Versailles, but since 1945 its cogency is evidenced, for example, by the articles on strategy and American world policy in *Foreign Affairs* and by the fact that the book has been reprinted several times, culminating in the Norton edition of 1962, edited by an American political scientist at Harvard. This book is one of the great services of the regional concept to the understanding of world strategy, and particularly of the confrontation of the Soviet Union vis-à-vis the powers of the United States and NATO. The plane and the bomb, it is claimed, make Mackinder's geostrategic view obsolete. This is clearly untrue. The confrontations in the Middle East and the Mediterranean, in Viet Nam, Taiwan, Korea, and Czechoslovakia, reveal a chain of hot spots in the transition zone between continental land power and engirdling sea and air power that is as effective, though changed in its potential technology, as it was 50 years ago,

This is no place to recapitulate in detail Mackinder's thesis. The reader is referred to the book in its recent paperback edition. His main basic concepts should, however, be stated here, so that the reader may at once grasp their significance.

The lands of the earth are grouped into one vast continental area, comprising Asia, Europe, and Africa. This Mackinder called the World Island. Around it are grouped the separate "islands" of North and South America, Australia, and the tiny offshore groups of the British and Japanese Islands. The World Island has witnessed through history, and particularly in the last 200 years with the emergence of large and strong imperial powers, the conflict of two trends. The core of the World Island, is the domain of the landsman. The coastlands are the potential domain of the seaman. Heartland and coastland were originally (1904) defined in terms of the area of inland drainage of central asia. This was later extended to embrace the river basins of eastern Europe that drain into the Baltic and Black Seas. Finally (1919), in thinking of modern geostrategy, Mackinder included lands that can be controlled by land power in eastern Europe (including the Baltic and Black Seas) and the Middle East, and the areas which can be controlled by sea power on the periphery. The zone of contact and conflict is an almost continuous belt, including the "belt of political change" in central Europe, reaching from Finland through Czechoslavakia to Greece; the Middle East; the northwest frontier passes to India, now controlled politically by Pakistan; the southeast Asian mainland, with Viet Nam as its major seat of current conflict; Taiwan; Korea; and the Japanese Islands.

British sea power prevented Russian land power throughout the nineteenth century from breaking through the Dardanelles. Now that its strength has waned, the Western Powers are confronted with the emergence of Russia as both a military power and (since World War II) as a sea power with unfettered entrance into the Mediterranean and, indeed, to all the coastlands of the World Island. The strategic situation in Korea in the 1950's was like that of the British in Crimea in the 1850's; American sea power was used against the military power of the Chinese as the land power. In Viet Nam, as doesn't seem to be too widely recognized, the sea power of the United States is confronted by Soviet technology, and equipment, that reaches northern Viet Nam by sea. In other words, the Soviet Union is today a sea power second only in strength to the United States in the Mediterranean, the Indian Ocean and the Western Pacific. This is the major geostrategic shift in the thesis formulated by Mackinder.

The atom bomb is a last resort. The localized conflicts of Korea, Viet Nam, and the support in defense given by the United States and NATO in order to contain Russian expansion reveal clearly the persistent validity of Mackinder's dictum. In these days of air power, it is possible to reach the Heartland by plane. Bases, rather than being sited on the mainland periphery, can be sited on islands on the Indian Ocean and the western Pacific, whence geostrategically the Heartland can be reached without transcending the rights and susceptibilities of the lesser states in the peripheral zone of contact and shattering on the mainland.

Currently, the NATO powers seek the containment of the Soviet Union in this zone. The Soviets, however, are competing, and steadily increasing their strength at sea and largely indirectly by economic and technical assistance, to the lesser states within it.

The concept of Mackinder has been of remarkable significance in the trends of world geostrategy, in spite of the changes brought about (potentially so) by the advent of new naval vessels, the plane, satellite, and the atom bomb. Not only the location of the world's hot spots are given a new meaning by this worldwide regional concept. Meaning is also given to the "cold war," the confrontation of the land powers of Russia and China, the efforts at containment (largely by assistance to lesser and weaker states in the zone of conflict), and the replacement of British naval and military and economic commitments by the extended sea arm of the United States. All these developments when viewed geostrategically on a map or globe are given a new meaning and significance when viewed in the light of the World Island, and its division into a Heartland and Peripheral Coastlands.

6. THE GEOGRAPHY OF FREEDOM

The world is divided regionally in its political associations and attitudes. These divisions are associations of states or dependent territories and also of peoples across the frontiers of states who have similar attitudes and aspirations that somehow must be met in a world of rising political expectations. The world seeks ways to freedom, certainly as one of the goals of the charter on human rights of the United Nations. The measures of freedom, however, in all its forms vary enormously and some of these geographic distributions are of profound geostrategic significance.

Freedom means freedom from want; freedom of speech; freedom from disease and from malnutrition; freedom in the exercise of civil and political rights. All aim at the welfare and happiness of the individual. Measures of freedom may be selected and their geographic distribution determined. There are great variations, for example, in longevity, the incidence of disease and the distribution of medical services, of diets, and illiteracy. To this list may be added the do's and dont's associated with particular religious and social groups. Poverty, as measured by diet, housing, or available work, afflicts at least two-thirds of the world's peoples. This is very unevenly distributed throughout the world and is most widespread in the less developed states. Personal freedom means the exercise of free speech and political rights, and these rights vary greatly and are particularly restricted in states with communistic or authoritarian systems. The demands and needs for capital in investment and modern technical equipment are also widely variable from one state to another and are particularly urgent matters in the new states. The countries of North America and Western Europe, as well as the Soviet Union and China, have extended offerings of technical aid and financial help well beyond their own frontiers.

These associations and varied geographic distributions, when mapped out, reveal three major distributions that are of great significance in world affairs.

The first is the marked concentration of aid, in all its forms, in the transion zone between the Heartland and the Coastlands of the World Island. This has had its greatest manifestation in the provision of aid to Western Eurpoe under the original provisions of the Marshall Plan.

A second characteristic is the concentration of massive financial aid and technical assistance in the poorer lands in inter-tropical latitudes. This includes the states of Latin America, and the group of new states in Africa, and the new states of southeastern Asia. Trade and aid between these less developed areas and the technically advanced and wealthy nations of the middle latitudes, both in the southern and northern hemispheres, is one of the major features of the world situation and will become of increasing significance and urgency in the coming generation.

The third geographic distribution is associated with the eclipse over the past 10 years of the two dominant world powers, the United States and the Soviet Union. Not only statistics of growth, but also geographic patterns of world trade and the distribution of financial and technical aid, reveal two rapidly growing world groupings that will increasingly act as a counterbalance to the policies and counsels of the first two. These are the West European group, which is being increasingly dominated by Germany; and the East Asian group in which Japan, in different ways from before World War II, is steadily and inevitably resuming its role as the leader of an East Asian Co-prosperity Sphere. Such are the geostrategic realities of our changing and divided world.

7. REGIONAL DEVELOPMENT

It is appropriate to examine the utility of the regional concept in the diagnosis and treatment of practical problems of contemporary society. There are numerous investigations of this kind, as has already been indicated in previous chapters. I list a few examples. Many years ago a leading geographer in Britain and another in France worked out suggestions for new regional divisions for their respective countries that might serve as a more effective framework for responsible self-government than the outmoded counties and departments. Fawcett's book on 'The Natural Provinces of England' (1919) is still so cogent to current problems that it has recently been reprinted, with later statistics, but no change of text (1961). Vidal de la Blache's scheme in 1910 is still unresolved in France, for De Gaulle's proposal for implementing a system of regional government was rejected in April 1969 by the electorate. Scholars have become more preoccupied with social service in the last two decades. In my early days such a preoccupation was widely regarded as beneath the concern of the scholar. There are now available for example, studies of the regional variants of "economic health" in New York State, of income in Britain, and of living levels throughout India. There are measurements of the potential agricultural capacity of different categories of land in various countries. An atlas is devoted to maps of the world by states of what is somewhat dubiously called "economic development."

The key question to all of these enquiries is the determination of regional variants of modes of living. They raise two questions, especially in under-developed areas with dominantly agrarian societies. First, what are the existing levels of living and how can they be measured - by cash income, food-intake (calories per day per person), or available work per agricultural worker? Second, what are the measurable prospects of betterment in terms of the regional variants of land and opportunity? The acid test of the regional approach is to determine and explain, and recommend action upon the regional variants of socio-economic conditions of agricultural workers, whether in cash, work, food, or access to civilized amenities in village and town.

The problem of regional development is a matter of urgent concern not only to the "less developed" countries, but also to the "most advanced" countries in the world, notably the United States and Western Europe. Poverty, malnutrition, underemployment, and inadequate housing and schools prevail, in varying degree, in Appalachia and the Deep South, to say nothing of substantial sectors of every big city. Western Europe has a great diversity of regional levels of living. Britain has its "under-developed" moorlands in Wales and Scotland, often remote from the amenities of modern living. It has extensive obsolescent or drab industrial areas with sub-normal rates of economic growth. France has poor and disorganized sections in the south and west. Norway has its remote regions of environmental difficulties and social inadequacies, north of Trondheim. Germany has its sub-normal border zones along the iron curtain. Italy has its *over*-developed lands in the south, with too many people, needing more jobs and better expectations. Belgium has areas that need priority of treatment, in the outworn, old, coalmining area of Mons-Charleroi and the textile manufacturing areas of Flanders in its north-western corner. All these cases reveal clearly the great regional variations in socioeconomic structure, that demand thorough assessment and remedial action with high priority in order to provide all people within the state with a socially acceptable standard of living.

Rather than indulge in further general discussion of these questions, and protagonism of the theory and objectives of such remedial studies in under-developed areas, I refer the reader to my case study of a notorious poverty-stricken area in southern Italy. I refer to the mainland of southern Italy, where a mammoth program of regional development was embarked upon by the central government 20 years ago. My choice of the area was encouraged by the fact that the Italian

Census is a remarkable fund of statistical information for every individual commune. Agricultural economists have also produced many exhaustive regional monographs on agrarian conditions based on specific and exact family budgets. My study began in the early fifties. It preceded the government's program of regional development and revealed the urgency of the demand for aid. My work continued in the early sixties in an appraisal of the differentially distributed problems of economic growth and social betterment that have confronted the program since its inception.[3]

The purpose of these studies was to locate nearly three hundred small agrarian units, each of which consisted of a group of communes, that were similar in agrarian structure. Within this frame, I classified and mapped the major kinds of terrain; agriculture; the degree of clustering of farms, villages, and hamlets; levels of income per family; and days of available work per worker (based on accepted estimates of workdays per acre demanded by various kinds of crop or livestock). These evaluations were made for about 1950. The regional variants in economic and social structure and their associated problems of rehabilitation, such as size of holdings, permanence of tenures, agricultural practices, irrigation, improved marketing facilities, new industrial plants and housing, are measured and mapped for each of the areas. The impact is examined over the 20 years that have elapsed since the government initiated its large program of regional development.

[3]Published in English in *Heidelberger Studien zur Kulturgeographie: Festgabe für Gottfried Pfeifer, Heidelberg Geographische Arbeiten,* 1966. A monograph entitled *The Population Problem of Southern Italy: An Essay in Social Geography* was published by Syracuse University Press, 1955, 116 pages (out of print).

Chapter 11

THE REGIONAL CONCEPT IN EDUCATION

1. OBSERVATION TO GENERALIZATION

Observation of the world around is one of the inborn curiosities of the human. Formal education seeks to cultivate this curiosity for the fuller enjoyment of life's course. The regional concept, if properly presented and taught, contributes richly to this goal, for it is based throughout on the educational principle of proceeding from the known to the unknown, from the particular observation in the visible landscape or townscape to the generalization, from the local visual scene, viewed through a window or on a walk, to imagined world patterns. Running water after a heavy rain, a dry channel, the growth of a plant, rocks, soils, hedges, walls, buildings, streets, verges and ornamental trees, telegraph poles, garbage cans are for all to see as part of the environment. The regional concept starts from such individual elements of the visible scene and seeks to find which of them are spatially repetitive. This creates an awareness of the spatial arrangement and association of things in the landscape. It helps us to reject what is not appropriate or fitting. It is a way of looking at the world around that helps cultivate an aesthetic sense. In a world of urban ugliness, such observant and critical attitudes are woefully deficient. They should be trained throughout the high school, the University, as, indeed, throughout life.

A major change in education in Britain was brought about by a series of lectures given to young people in London in 1869 by T. H. Huxley, the distinguished natural scientist and ardent follower of the evolutionary views of his colleague, Charles Darwin. These lectures were published in 1878 with the title *Physiography: An Introduction to the Study of Nature.* Huxley chose this term, that was previously used in the study of minerals, in order to distinguish it from "physical geography." Studies of physical geography, he declared, "begin at the wrong end, and too often terminate in an *omnium gatherum* of scraps of all sorts of undigested and uncorrected information, thereby entirely destroying the educational value of that study which Kant justly termed the propaedeutic of natural knowledge." Huxley started his lectures with the immediately accessible surroundings of the children in the London area rather than with abstract principles. He thus applied a basic principle of the educative process, that proceeds from the known to the unknown. This educational principle is true of the world of Nature and of the works of Man, and it is as apt today as it was a hundred years ago.

The process of learning also demands that much must be learned by memory. This is an unpopular attitude in a world where the pedagogical approach is currently dominated by the idea that everything should be tied in to a pattern or generalization which the small child supposedly can understand. We believe this to be absolutely untrue of the learning process. It is because education gives no attention to the discipline of memorizing of places and states, and where they are and their dominant characteristics that the overwhelming majority of teen-agers in American universities are geographically illiterate. Geography, indeed, has virtually disappeared from the school syllabus in the U. S. A. This presents every college teacher with a formidable problem, for we must *all* learn where places are and the teacher in school and college must devise motivation and method for teaching them facts. Where is Viet Nam or Korea? What is the significance of its location? What is the pattern and the associated names of the states of the United States? What is the approximate population (in broad categories) of the world's (major) states? This ignorance of place among a people that is involved in worldwide commitments, social, financial, and strategic, in nothing short of tragic and needs to be put right both in high school and university.

This leads to another point, the aesthetic attitude towards the physical world. The environment has all sorts of unfathomed reactions on the individual, the family, and the society. The world of Nature, vast plains, forbidding mountains, the blazing heat of the desert, the vagaries of the weather, have direct impacts on human mentality. The modes of impact and interpretation of environment have somehow to blend with the attitudes of the people concerned. People in different cultures perceive and interpret Nature in different ways. The physical world as well as the *mores* of its people cannot be measured quantitatively. They must be observed, recorded, and interpreted qualitatively. The media needed for such expression are the painting, the poem, and the novel. This is the meaning of the adjective "regional" that is often used in this connection. One of the most remarkable essays on the environmental interpretation of art was due to Alexander von Humboldt in *Cosmos* over a hundred years ago. Such creative writings express the distinctive regional quality of a land and its people as envisaged and expressed by its observers and aesthetic recorders.

We must find ways and means of training a sense of appreciation and rejection of what is undesirable in the landscape. It is easy for humans to accept ugliness around them, be it in the drabness of the Victorian towns of Britain, or the masses of unsightly overhead wires and poles that besmirch the grandeur of the Catalina Mountains in Tucson. Aesthetic taste is easily dulled and the educational system is largely responsible.

The use of the environs as a medium for learning is one of the oldest and soundest principles of teaching. This was the essential of the German principle known as *Heimatkunde* practiced in the teaching of small children right through the educative process (both formal and informal). It uses the local and real environment within reach of the school as the source of learning, of observing, recording and explaining, whether it be learning about Nature or learning of the work and works of Man. The economies of eastern Asia or wheat cultivation in Australia should begin with rice pudding or daily bread on the table at home. Personal observation and experience should precede abstract generalization for both young and old. This is the purpose of the regional concept. It begins with outdoors and contact with the real world and its infinite offerings. First generalizations are reached inductively from the particular, and in the case of the regional concept, they are concerned with the spatial or environmental groupings of contiguous places, from the doorstep or the street to the world pattern. Knowledge, understanding, and critical evaluation of the spatial interrelations of places are its objectives.

2. REGIONAL SURVEY: PATRICK GEDDES AND AFTER

The regional concept was formulated and practiced by Patrick Geddes and his devotees in Britain under the title of "regional survey." It had profound repercussions on education as well as on community planning. This impact was particularly strong in the land of its birth; it had a negligible impact on the United States. For this very reason it should be given special emphasis, for it is of profound significance, but widely neglected, in our contemporary American society.

The teaching of geography in school and university in Britain felt the effects of Geddes insistence on field observation and map representation. His principles and procedures were put on record in a remarkable small museum in an old building near the castle, the Outlook Tower, in Edinburgh. This began with locally observed data on the first floor, and an increasingly wide area of representation, ending with the world, on upper floors. On the roof was a "camera obscura" where, in a dark room, the city of Edinburgh and its environs were reflected on a plane surface. The new departments of geography in the universities (largely through the teaching of A. J. Herbertson, who was an early junior colleague of Geddes) focused on field work and map study. The deterministic chain of cause and effect, working from the environment at base, continued to be used, however, as the framework of teaching and thinking. Geography was then regarded (as this writer can personally testify) as an assembly of various fields of knowledge, and it was considered to be beneath intellectual dignity to question its distinctive battery of concepts or its unique and distinctive purposes in the realm of knowledge.

The emphasis on field work in the learning process has continued to this day in Britain. Geddes derived the essentials of his conceptual procedures in "regional survey" from the work of Frederic Le Play, the French scholar. The Leplay Society, emerged some 40 years ago in London from the Sociological Society, with which Geddes was so closely associated. It sought "a regional survey" at first hand on the lines established by Geddes, over a period of several weeks in areas occupied by "rustic" societies, removed from the complicating impact of modern urbanism. Such areas (on which reports were published) were Slovenia, Sardinia, and Corsica. Broader cursory tours under expert guidance, were among the educational achievements of this society, in which this writer took part in the thirties as both participant and leader. Special attention also was given to observation and training in selected areas in Britain. My first experience in leading such a group was to sort out some 30 people (mostly teachers) with a diversity of interests and skills into groups of three or four which could undertake some manageable task of field study in the allotted time. It so happened that the area, Les Eyzies, Dordogne, is one of the classic sites of prehistoric finds, so that the activity of the group was inevitably, directed to this theme with the guidance of a famous local French expert. There was no focal expertise or interest, and it was on the spot that groups were made among the participants. The results of this field work were published in 1932.[1]

This procedure, with substantial modifications to meet the attitudes of changing times, remains basic to the training of all those involved in field studies—zoologists, botanists, geologists, geographers. It is normal for a group of undergraduates in these fields in a British university to spend seven to ten days in the field in an area at one headquarters in their first, second and third years of study.

Increasing attention is being given to field studies in Britain. The Society for the Promotion of Field Studies now owns ten centers that are used by schools and universities for residence and tuition and field headquarters for studies in the surrounding area. These studies are conducted by the professors of the groups and also by resident wardens. Most of the field work is undertaken in groups of three or four, on foot with map and notebook in hand. There are also about a dozen hostels of the Youth Hostels Association that are made available for

[1]Both the institute of Sociology (Le Play House) and the Le Play Society ended their days in 1955 and 1960 respectively. The Sociological Society (Le Play House) was founded in 1902 by Geddes in association with Victor Branford. Its periodical, *Sociological Review*, is still in publication.

such purposes, and well over a hundred residential centers, accomodating up to 50, are operated for school use by the Local Education Authorities.

Such is the application of the regional concept in education. It must be noted, however, that in both America and Britain a crisis has been reached, for there are far too many students for this kind of individual attention. New methods must be devised in order to adapt changed circumstances to the pedagogical demands. Buses and megaphones and crowds of a hundred or more in a class are emphatically no answer to this problem. Tuition must of necessity rest with individual assignments that involve field observation in areas accessible to the place of study.

3. IN SCHOOL

I recently had occasion to ask a class of American students (from various areas of study) a series of questions to find out their "standards of reference" that were relevant to a certain theme—the physical structure—geographic limits—of a city. I could get no answers to the following questions: What is the scale of your automobile road map? What are the approximate dimensions of a block? How many yards and feet in a mile? What is the length of a kilometer and how does it compare with a mile? How many square yards in an acre? What is a quarter section? How many townships in a mid-western county? How do you locate the south at midday? In what part of your horizon does the sun rise and set and how does this vary through the year? What kind of trees are dominant in the woodland in a valley two miles distant from the campus? How do you recognize a cottonwood, a maple, an oak? The class had no standards of reference, and therefore could give no answers to such fundamental questions about the world around.

The position in the education system of the United States is serious with regard to the development and sharpening of curiosity about the environment, apart from the location of gas stations and banks. Even distances in the remote country far from cities are often estimated in blocks. There is evidently no attempt to arouse or develop natural curiosity in high school, and the faculties in the universities consider such tuition to be beneath their dignity or patience. There is, thus, on the part of the overwhelming majority of citizens, a lack of aesthetic or practical appreciation (and thus of approval or disapproval) of the world around. British educators are actively aware of this pedagogical problem and seem (albeit without a great measure of success!) to gear their teaching procedures to it. The number of students (at all levels) is positively no excuse for avoiding these issues. New methods have to be devised for reaching the goal. At high school in Britain (admittedly a very unusual case, due to the dedication of a fine headmaster), I had to record each day through each year in a personal graph book, the daily fluctuations of temperature, wind, and rainfall. These measurements were taken personally in rotation, either from an instrument, or from winds and clouds. Walks with the teacher called for observation of trees, grasses, walls, houses, and the estimation of distances (how far from here to that distant barn?) and areas (how many acres in that field?). The same kind of questions can be posed and answered in the blocks around a school in a big city. Is there any repetitive pattern in the location of banks, stores, and schools? What is the size of these lots? What is the width of this street? Why are there deep dips on a road in the desert areas of southern Arizona? These questions help to develop standards of environmental reference. Such elementary basic instruction should be required of *all* freshmen in institutions of higher education. It should be taught in high school, but obviously it is not.

4. IN UNIVERSITY

In the education of a young freshman one can safely assume nothing. One must start from fundamental terms of observational references as Huxley did in seeking generalizations from the phenomena of Nature's work on the land.

Two kinds of introduction are needed for freshmen, an introductory course and a basic course for further training. Through no fault of theirs, students are the victims of the educational procedures in high school, and passive occupants and users of their environment of buildings, roads, and spaces. Some kind of general introductory course is necessary to overcome these appalling gaps. The teacher must select content, devise procedures, and discover motivation among his students. For what is needed is treatment of places and areas of the most fundamental kind that must have motivation in order to commit to memory. Also there is need to instill an approach and attitude in regard to the locale, context, and extent of man and landscape. The topics should include the reading of a map (scales, contours); the movements of the sun and the seasons; the role of a place as a focus of activity; the meaning of land use, learned by means of simple individual field exercises in town or country; basic world distributions of population by density by states; world distribution of cities; and, mapping by states of their modes of government and levels of living. All this is aimed at developing basic standards of reference, with regard to the local scene by daily observation, and the world location of lands, states and peoples by the study of maps. Such a course must somehow reach a compromise between memory learning, visual observation, and pedagogical motivation.

The first year of study in the university should be a General Survey Year. The student is introduced, in a manner different from that of the high school, to the field of human knowledge. Its purpose should be to cultivate interests and hopefully to whet the appetite. This is, in part, therefore, a major responsibility for the senior scholars of the university. In this endeavor, a course in Field Studies is essential. This should aim not only at the perceptual appreciation of the immediate world around, but also at a rational conceptual view of world affairs. This is a must for *all* students, who make up, be it recalled, up to 50 percent of the nation's youth. The education of such large numbers of young persons calls for experiment, for this is the commitment of the American ideal of universal education. It is necessary to help offset the blindness to the natural world and to the man-made environment, that seems to be engendered by the urban way of life and limitless stretches of concrete and asphalt.

I now turn to training in the regional concept. The following is a personal proposition, based upon experience and conviction. It is not a prescription for others, but fundamentals presented here are, in my view, the essentials for the training of any undergraduate in the field. Distinctive areas of specialization would come at the graduate levels and will depend on the interest of the professorial faculty.

The first year of study (the second year in the university) will contain three courses each of which will run through the whole session. The first course concerns the human elements of the regional concept; the second, the physical elements of the regional concept; and the third, the basic techniques—cartographic, statistical, and field. The first will deal with the definition and illustration of concepts of the spatial organization of human groups and their transformation of the natural landscape to the human environment. A suggested outline is given in the appendix. The second deals with the characteristics and formative processes of the physical earth. It will therefore embrace climates, landforms, hydrology, vegetation, and soils. The third will be a series of simple exercises in the laboratory covering two to three hours per week. It will cover the reading and interpretation of topographic maps, the mapping of statistical data, and some elementary instruction with exercises on statistical techniques of areal analysis.

Ancillary courses in other disciplines will be necessary. I suggest two social sciences (general economics, sociology, anthropology) and two natural sciences (geology, botany, physics, mathematics).

In the following years, without specifying the sequence, there should be further development of the introductory courses. These would be as follows:

1. Human Elements. The Geography of Settlement; Economic Geography; Social Geography; Political Geography; Cultural Geography.
2. Physical Elements. Geomorphology; Climatology; Biogeography; Hydrology and Oceanography.
3. Techniques. This laboratory course should continue through the whole course of study. It will be devoted to the interpretation of topographic maps, the preparation of maps of areally distributed data (e.g., rainfall, population, crop data), and the preparation and interpretation of weather maps.
4. ONE Major Area. The student should be required to take one or two courses in one major world area, so as to have a reasonable competence and understanding of the operation and meaning of the regional concept.

This course of study should be accompanied by a careful choice of supporting courses in one or two other disciplines. Suggestions for this choice would be botany (plant ecology); anthropology (cultural or physical anthropology); sociology (rural and urban ecology); geology (structural geology); or atmospheric physics (meteorology).

5. SUMMARY OF BASIC REGIONAL CONCEPTS

The regional concept, as expounded in these pages, embraces subsidiary concepts all of which should be formulated as the basis of training at all levels. Such an aim is achieved through lectures from the lectern and exercises in the laboratory. The concepts may be listed as follows. This framework is fundamental, but frequently ignored or hidden by a facade of intellectual expertise. The meaning of each concept should be clearly defined so that we are aware of the battery of concepts we seek to develop. I am entirely opposed to the current trend of specialized training in special fields before one is familiar with the relevant disciplines. Fifteen sub-concepts may be summarized as follows from the preceding chapters.

1. *The regional concept* refers to the processes whereby phenomena associate on the earth's surface in spatial groupings, physical, biotic, or human. Such groupings may be unique (e.g., the Deep South) or generic (e.g., a type of economy or a type of climate or vegetation). The distinctive human characteristics of such a grouping contain three groups of components: (1) repetitive spatial adaptations of human occupance to the terrain; (2) symbiotic or interconnected relations of one place with another; and (3) innovations that at some time entered into and were absorbed (or rejected!) into a human-spatial complex. This approach, though applicable to plant and animal associations, has reference in this context to the land and its biotic cover strictly interpreted in its relevance to human use. The total physical environment is interpreted, in content and problems, in terms of human groups, in the light of their purpose in occupying a given piece of land, their inherited attitudes (which may be brought with them from another milieu), and the technical equipment at their disposal. This is the basic springboard for all geographic enquiry.
2. *The concept of space relations or location.* This refers to the location of places, however defined, in relation to other places of the same kind, be this a local area, a major portion of the earth's surface, or the whole of the earth's surface. It refers, therefore, essentially to astronomical position (latitude and longitude), with which are associated diurnal variations, seasons, and time. It also refers to location in relation to the distribution of land and water, and in relation to physical and human characteristics of adjacent

areas. It also has deep significance in relation to the character, conditions, and problems of states. The significance of location in all these respects varies through time according to changing technics, attitudes, and group policies and objectives (in war, peace and diplomacy). Several of the concepts listed below, have emerged from this fundamental geographic idea.

3. *The concept of site or terrain* refers to physical characteristics of terrain—relief, depth of water table, surface run-off, flood, subsurface materials, vegetation, temperature variations, insolation—evaluated in terms of human use. The concept of site as a local area with a composite distinctive association of physical characteristics (as opposed to abstractions represented by contours, isohyets, etc.) was adopted by plant ecologists (in Britain) in the thirties. It has been a standard concept for a hundred years, and has been an important field of investigation, notably in Germany, during the past 20 years or so.

Every area is a mosaic of sites or terrains that present the essential base for human use. These need to be mapped and evaluated in order to determine the potentials and problems of human occupance. This is essential, for example, to land planner, urban planner, realtor, and architect. Such an approach is needed in much of the traditional division of "physical geography" into a number of special fields which now stand alone: geomorphology; climatology; oceanography; pedology; and biogeography.

4. *The concept of centrality* (or nodality) holds that the services needed by the population of an area tend to segregate at fixed places, which places exhibit recognizable regularities of grade and spacing, depending on the density of population, occupational structure, level of living, and culture, of the areas in which they are located.

5. *The concept of the socio-economic base* holds that the locale of a fixed place (or settlement) rests upon certain activities that bring income into it. These activities are called basic. Activities that support the basic workers and their families are non-basic. A basic-non-basic ratio, that lies at the root of urban growth, can be measured in any area, urban or rural, though the procedure is complicated.

6. *The concept of the regional base* of a fixed place is closely related to the idea of centrality and the basic-non-basic ratio. Every

service (e.g., a supermarket or doctor) and institution (e.g., a primary school) must be strategically located in relation to its catchment area. Every central place, be it hamlet, village, townlet, town, city, or metropolis, emerges through the assembly of such services and institutions. It also develops, like a magnetic field, a seat of centrifugal and centripetal forces, that bring it into close connection with the surrounding area. Herein lie the concepts of the urban field, hinterland, city region, milk-shed, labor-shed, journey-to-work area.

7. *The concept of the threshold* refers to the minimum spatial requirements needed for the effective operation of a localized function together with the area it seeks to serve and organize. As a current practical example, a school needs a certain minimum number of pupils, rooms, and staff, and, therefore, a certain number children of approximate school-going age in order to function effectively, and it must also have effective access to an adequate catchment area. These considerations apply to all service institutions in our modern society. They are also basic to the spatial configuration of states and their subdivisions throughout history in terms of the functions of the capital and its access (time and distance) to its frontiers and to its effectively settled parts. This is a locational factor that is measurable in relation to a "threshold." It is applicable to the initial delineation of township, county, and state, and is an essential criterion in any intentions of territorial reorganization.

8. *The concept of the functional area.* There is a basic and universal tendency for people and institutions to segregate in space. The spatial fabric of a city is arranged in several orders (see p. 140). The modes of segregation of shopping centers and the extent and content of the "central business district" have been subjected to detailed analysis on these lines. There is need for much more thorough diagnosis on these lines in order to more effectively reconstruct urban areas. Above all, such segregations must be interpreted dynamically, that is in terms of growth and change through time.

9. *The concept of the urbanized area* is another challenging geographic concept that urgently needs attention. How can this urban association be measured? What are the processes involved? What are the desirable limits and what remedial measures should be

taken? The impact of Gottmann's work on *Megalopolis* indicates the significance of these questions.

10. *The concept of regional development.* Concepts of areal differentials in levels of living, economic health, and resource development, are of fundamental significance at both the national and international scales and they are intimately associated with the growth and spread of urbanism. Government action must recognize the significance of regional variants of social and economic conditions that demand differential treatment, rather than blanket legislation for all sectors of the state.

11. *The concept of regional consciousness.* This refers to the tendency of groups in particular areas to have a consciousness of togetherness. This embraces measurable associations of trade, political aspirations, and cultural heritage. It also includes many regional names and terrain types (in local areas) that are referred to by name by the indigenous people and their forerunners.

12. *The concept of the morphology of the human habitat.* The physical forms of groundplan and build of human settlements are spatially repetitive, depending on their functions and historical development. Physical forms are the individual component structures of the habitat—streets, buildings, spaces, monuments. Grouping refers to the spatial arrangement of these forms in a single place and this, in large measure, is culturally determined. The habitat, in this sense, is studied by many specialists. Regional enquiry searches for the distribution of the forms and other associated phenomena. The study of field systems, of woodlands and their places in the landscape, of farmsteads, villages and towns as cultural forms and as items of the cultural landscape, has long been an established and respected field of enquiry in France and Germany.

13. *The concept of sequent occupance.* Human groups, through the heritage of habits, attitudes, and technical skills, make an impact on the landscape in transforming it as their habitat. A sequence of several groups through time is reflected in transformations in the landscape and in the survival of many vestigial remnants, distinct in form and location. As an example, buildings are erected as "cultural forms" to carry out specific functions. However, with the passing of time, the form may be transformed as its function changes, and may eventually be demolished and replaced

by a new form designed (to the best of the architect's ability) to serve a new function. In terms of the spatial segregation of people, this process has been expressed by urban ecologists as dominance (i.e., one group dominates and seeks to exclude intrusion), invasion (i.e., the entrance of new groups), and succession (i.e., the new invasive groups ultimately become dominant). The regional concept, starting with individual spatial elements in the urban habitat, seeks to discover how they segregate and the processes involved in locale and limits.

14. *The concept of the origin and spread of innovations.* The origin, development and unequal geographic spread of human innovations, and, in consequence, the differential roles they play in human spatial complexes, has long been a primary concern of students of human societies. Innovations embrace ideas and techniques that have emerged and spread in the remote past (e.g., domesticated plants and animals, methods of irrigation, the plow and the hoe, milking, the two and four wheeled cart, draft-animals). Innovations also embrace in our own day the spread and exact present distribution of radio, of hybrid corn, of milch cattle and drinking milk. The acceptance and areal spread of such "technical" aid to pre-industrial societies often meets with the resistance of human groups in particular areas, to which the innovations are not acceptable because of taboos on food, the treatment of animals, or the diminutive size of subsistence holdings.

15. *The concept of a cultural region.* This is an area in which the people have an association of common cultural traits—habits, attitudes, religious beliefs, speech, implements, etc. It was first developed by cultural anthropologists in America in reference to the pre-Columbian Indian cultures of North America. It is similarly applicable to post-industrial societies throughout the world.

A pause is needed to be more specific about the meaning of this last concept. The fullest recent exposition, as to procedures and content, is in Ralph Linton's *Tree of Culture.* This is a major historical interpretation of the theaters of localization of pre-industrial cultures. This would serve as the substance and text of an advanced course, but its essential concepts should be introduced as soon as possible. As introductory works we would name (as we have used in freshman courses) the following: Sauer's *Origins and Dispersals;* Hettner's *Gang der Kultur über die Erde:* and the more recent world-view of human cultures by Hans Bobek; now available in English (with map) in Wagner and Mikesell, *Readings in Cultural Geography.* The last work should be a basic frame of reference, a "human base," that is as essential as the "physical base" in the study of regionalism. Several text-books define the world's major cultural realms. The major characteristics and distribution of these realms should be required in an introductory course which could then serve as a springboard for the more advanced courses in later years.

This whole conceptual framework has been based for over 40 years, as far as I am concerned, on the early writings in the twenties of Carl Sauer *(Morphology of Landscape)* and Lewis Mumford *(Sticks and Stones).* Attention is drawn to these and their later works for guidance as to the distinctive qualities of regional thought.

6. THE PROSPECT

I now briefly turn in conclusion to ways and means of promoting research and application of the regional concept. In general, I find myself in close agreement with E. Ackerman.[2] He suggests that research should be concentrated on the spatial impact of processes in the physical, biotic, and cultural realms. I repeat, however, that the objective of such work should be the understanding of *geographic complexes.* This means how, where, and why they localize, develop, and spread over the earth, as a whole, the major parts, or the smallest segments. The study of particular processes must be subordinated, and relative aspects selected or pursued, to this end. As Carl Ritter, the modern founder of the regional concept, insisted over a hundred years ago, the whole circle of sciences must be drawn upon, but subordinated to the single objective of regional characterization of associations of phenomena over the earth.

The fields of future research thus lie in directions noted in the previous paragraph. On the physical side, three aspects call for canalized attention. First, the work of erosion and earth-movements in the development, types and distribution of the physical forms of the earth's surface; second, the processes involved in the development, types, and distribution of plant formations, or, more comprehensively,

[2]Ackerman, E. A., *Geography as a Fundamental Research Discipline,* University of Chicago, Research Paper, No. 53, 1958.

biotic complexes; and, third, the meteorological processes which average out as climatic conditions and their spatial variants. Study in each of these areas has clearly defined scientific objectives and special techniques of field observation and quantitative analysis. Current emphasis is being given to the study of a process as an end in itself. This may lead to highly significant discovery, but it does not contribute directly to promotion of the regional concept, on which much closer understanding is essential.

On the human side, which is the central concern of this bood, there is a plethora of detailed studies, but relatively few and fecund problems that challenge the attention of scholars in the realm of regionalization. We suggest that to achieve this end, attention should be focused on four areas. These are essentially ecological in kind and raise questions that are going to be of increasing concern in the life and organization of human societies in the coming decades.

1. The density, migrations, and distribution of population.
2. The organization of space and the use of land in terms of government, economic development (including capital investment and systems of management) and their varying impact from one area to another.
3. The areal impact of technical equipment and skills or innovations in particular geographic complexes on the utilization of resources and human welfare.
4. The areal impact of the conquest of distance, that is, communication.

A note is required on the fourth area. Modern techniques, such as new tools, crops, and rotations, may fit readily into an existing geographic complex, be it physical or socio-economic. They may indeed trigger off a number of other changes in the areas into which they are introduced. On the other hand, innovations in diet (such as eating flesh or drinking milk or wine) may be unacceptable to human groups in particular areas, the extent of which is only vaguely known. These techniques of communication, the "space-adjusting techniques" as Ackerman calls them, include (in our interpretation) the means of circulation; the interaction of centers of settlement upon each other in terms of their function, size and spacing; and the internal spatial structure of the city. The city grows in order to minimize the "friction of space" and should therefore seek to reduce the journey to work to a minimum—to work, shop, and school. New principles of planning are needed in place of customary "zoning" procedures, so as to group homes, spaces and institutions on some kind of community (or neighborhood) basis that will be both economically efficient and socially desirable.

Salient and meaningful objectives for the advancement of knowledge and social service lie in each of these fields. The regional concept and its expertise will contribute to the precise assessment of (1) areal distribution; (2) primary determinants; (3) associated elements; and (4) potentials of growth within distinctive geographic complexes. Study of the content and range of such complexes needs skilled procedures. These procedures are of three kinds; first, the use of maps of the earth, be they conventional two-dimensional topographic maps or small scale maps at the scale of an atlas; second, the use of quantitative procedures to measure, map, and interpret, terrestrial distributions and their associations; third, skill in the observation in the field, including the use of interview techniques. Decision-makers should know the special expertise of the regional concept as revealed by this list. To it, however, should be further added an intimate familiarity with one major area of the earth, and a real competence in the history and language of its peoples. This is a tall order, but such it is and must be.

The practical application of a concept and its expertise to regional development demands not merely more ex-cathedra planning by a social conscience on a nationwide scale from Whitehall or Washington; such as a Beeching on British railways, Buchanan on urban traffic in Britain, an economist advising Whitehall in London, or antipoverty specialists or urbanologists in Washington, D.C. It demands clear objectives in both philosophy and practice. It demands the expertise of skilled workers in the social sciences in institutes of higher learning. Training in the traditional fields of economics, political science, sociology, and geography is essential, but emphatically inadequate, although rigorous training in these disciplines is absolutely essential. It does not help much if an enquiry or directive from on high reaches such a department for individual attention. The department lacks, or has to learn, the expertise from others, and this is a wasteful process. There has long been talk of teamwork, but this is difficult to achieve over a short period. We need much more of it urgently. We need to bring disciplines more effectively together so as to employ their joint expertise to tackle problems concerned with human groups in their spatial arrangement and in the organization of the land they use. Scientific fragmentation hinders rather than helps further understanding and application of the regional concept to problems of social growth and environmental planning.

The present trend in Britain and in the United States is for the university to establish new departments or for research projects to reach specific departments. There is a spate of new departments of "City and Regional Planning." There are already departments of Environmental Planning. Ecology and conservation are also in the running, and some of their undergraduate courses seem to cover the waterfront of the natural and social sciences. There is certainly an appalling amount of duplication of effort in training and research. Departments, often with governmental support, are doing the things that their neighbors could do more effectively. There is also the perplexing question before a university takes the plunge—what can a department of planning do over and above what the established disciplines can do for it? I am not criticizing but underlining this trend and its problems, for it is apparently a step in the direction which I am discussing.

In conclusion, attention should be drawn to the report of a committee of the Earth Sciences Division of the National Academy of Sciences (1965). Excerpts from its summary of the concepts and methods of *The Science of Geography,* read as follows:

> "Geography treats the man-environment system primarily from the point of view of space in time. It seeks to explain how the sub-systems of the physical environment are organized on the earth's surface, and how Man distributes himself over the earth in his space relation to physical features and to other men. Geography's organizing concept, for which "spatial distributions and space relations" are a verbal shorthand, is a tri-scalar space. The scales comprise extent, density, and succession. Geography's theoretical framework is developed from this basic concept. Settlement (central place) hierarchy, density, thresholds, and diffusion theory, are examples of theoretical constructs serving specific research."

> "Geographers have long believed that correlations of spatial distributions are among the most ready keys to understanding existing

or developing life systems, social systems, or environmental changes. As geographers undertook such studies in the past they favored heavily the empirical-inductive method. More recently, particularly since the end of the last war, theoretical-deductive methods have been applied. The two currents of thought are now achieving a healthy balance within the research "clusters" that are on the "growing edge" of the field. . . ."

"The central section of the report attempts to analyze the interests and competences among geographers that contribute to inter-disciplinary progress in studying the great man-environment system. This analysis is presented in the form of discussions of four different problem areas considered illustrative of the growing edge of geography. The four problem areas are: physical geography, cultural geography, political geography, and location theory. Within each problem area one or more research clusters are found. These are groups with common research interests whose members habitually communicate with one another. For each problem area the Committee evaluates the significance of present and foreseeable research problems, the connection of current working problems with the great overriding problem of Man and Environment, the relation of the problem area to growing edges in other sciences, and research opportunities considered to be unfulfilled."

"The Committee is certain that, as settlement continues to become more dense in the world and in this nation, the arts of managing space efficiently will be ever more in demand and of ever greater economic importance. Geography seeks the fundamental knowledge that supports the space-managing arts, and contributes to satisfaction of scientific curiosity about the Man-Natural environment system. The recommended measures would strengthen a field that is on the threshold of some of its most effective work."

The approach of this book agrees with the opening paragraphs and the selected fields that are to be studied with respect to the regionalization of Man-Land relations. The Committee's views are virtually identical with those of Ackerman. They reflect current trends in the United States. They call for the following critical comments in the light of my presentation of the regional concept. The study of "spatial distributions" puts its emphasis on the analysis of individual geographic variables, rather than on the elucidation of spatial syndromes.

It certainly has led to a neglect (to use the Committee's own words) of "the physical environment" as "organized" by Man on "the earth's surface." Even more serious is the fact that no attention is given (in the four selected fields) to the association of these fields in particular areas of the world, nor to the search for specific Man-Land problems in particular areas emerging through time that add up to more than the summation of these four special fields. This arises from the current distrust in America of what is "unique" in an area, rather than what is "generic". The individuality of areas is an established objective of enquiry about Man-Land relations, and is the central motif of the regional concept. The purpose of this book has been to expound briefly and boldly the purpose and content of this concept both as a field of research and as a medium of education and of understanding public affairs. The reader may now be left to draw his own conclusions.

APPENDIX: AN INTRODUCTION TO THE REGIONAL CONCEPT

1. The Human Elements of the Regional Concept

This should consistently aim at the conceptual base, a local and first-hand illustration, and then a brief illustration of a hierarchical arrangement towards a worldwide classification and distribution.

Several lectures will be devoted to each topic, depending on time available. About 50 to 60 are assumed as a minimum. (i.e., two semesters).

The aim is principle not detail and one should not be daunted by the large scope of the coverage in either the human or the physical aspects.

2. The Development of the Regional Concept

Discussion of the meaning of definitions of content and purpose, from Strabo, to Ritter and Humboldt, Richthofen, Mackinder, Davis, and Vidal de la Blache and subsequent leaders.

3. The Conceptual Framework

In the light of changing procedures with changing philosophies over one hundred years of growth. Holism, Environmental Determinism, Possibilism, Ecology, Perception, Organization of Space.

4. The Human Habitat

The broad frame of the world's natural environments and the distribution of the settled lands and the types of human occupancy.

5. The Concept of Site

Specific examples and first-hand observation in the field.

a. The site unit as an ecotope.
b. The regional association of sites in a hierarchy of units.
c. The world pattern of major natural entities.

6. The Development and Spread of Human Technics

A historical perspective on the interpretation of the variants of human occupance in the light of technics. The frame of Lewis Mumford - eotechnic, paleotechnic, neotechnic, and biotechnic—and Carl Sauers [*Origins and Dispersals*.] Selected modern examples.

7. The Human Habitat

The concept explained and illustrated at first-hand.

a. The farmstead: structure and regional variants.

b. The field system and its associated farms and villages.

c. The town as a morphological complex of buildings, streets and spaces.

d. The urbanized area and the range of urbanization.

8. The Distribution of Population

a. The meaning of density in relation to natural resources and levels of living.

b. Localized examples, e.g., Iowa, Eastern England, a European case, Java, an Occidental city.

c. Regional differentials of demographic characteristics—life expectancy, disease, proportions of urban to rural, rates of growth.

9. The Cultural Complex

The concept explained and illustrated.

a. Origins and dispersal. Examples.

b. World classification and distribution of regional cultures—aim rather than content.

c. A world map of cultural realms.

10. The Social Complex

Habits, attitudes and associations of social groups in their regional variations.

a. Language.

b. Religion.

c. Literacy.

d. Legal Codes.

11. The Economic Complex

The concept explained as a spatial entity of economic activity and interrelations.

a. The agricultural complex. (Resource - Extracting Technics)

b. The industrial complex, spatial similarities and interlinkage. (Resource – Converting Technics)

c. The comercial complex. (Space-Adjusting Technics)

(1) The route and the route net. (2) The center and the hierarchy of places.

12. The Political Complex

The concept explained as an entity of political attitudes and organization.

a. Regional diversity and territorial unity within the State.

b. Policy as a geographic determinant.

c. Frontier.

d. Capital.

e. Distance, size and access in the organization of a political area —at the level of township, State, or Interstate association.

13. Regional Consciousness

The concept defined as awareness of territorial association.

a. Terrain nomenclature in local usage.

b. Regional names (e.g. [*pays, gau*]).

c. Ethnic associations (Scandinavia, Deutschland, French-Canada, Anglo-America).

d. World names—Old World, New World, Middle East, Western Europe, Atlantic Community.

INDEX